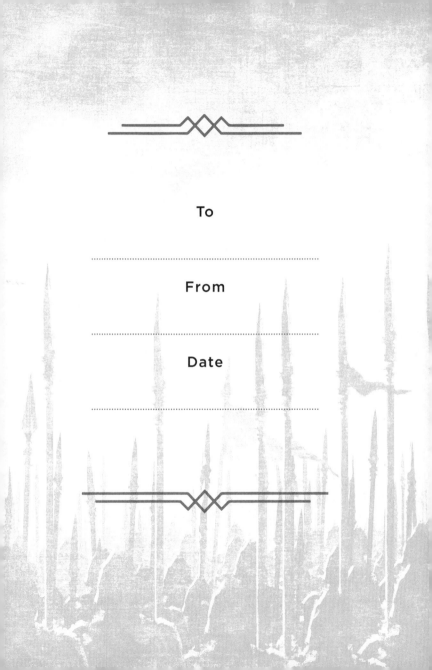

To

....

From

....

Date

....

MAN OF COURAGE

100 DEVOTIONS *for the* **FEARLESS LIFE**

GLENN HASCALL

BARBOUR
PUBLISHING

ISBN 978-1-63609-494-6

Published by Barbour Publishing, Inc., 1810 Barbour Drive, Uhrichsville, Ohio 44683, www.barbourbooks.com

Our mission is to inspire the world with the life-changing message of the Bible.

ecpa Member of the
Evangelical Christian
Publishers Association

Printed in China.

**Men, set a powerful example for the world.
Be the person God wants you to be
with *Man of Courage* devotions.**

Masculinity has come under fire in recent years, but the world needs Christian men like never before. *Man of Courage: 100 Devotions for the Fearless Life* celebrates men, the ones who pray boldly to God, speak truthfully to culture, and serve sacrificially in their families, churches, and communities.

Each entry encourages you to "be the man"—the man who

- steps up
- moves forward
- humbly resists
- believes in a miracle
- follows the King of courage.

You'll be challenged and encouraged to fill your God-given role in your home, your workplace, your community, and your world.

Be the Man
WHO STEPS UP

Again a message came to me from the LORD: "Son of man, give the people of Israel this message: In the day of my indignation, you will be like a polluted land, a land without rain. Your princes plot conspiracies just as lions stalk their prey. . . . Your priests have violated my instructions and defiled my holy things. . . . Even common people oppress the poor, rob the needy, and deprive foreigners of justice. I looked for someone who might rebuild the wall of righteousness that guards the land. I searched for someone to stand in the gap in the wall so I wouldn't have to destroy the land, but I found no one."

EZEKIEL 22:23-26, 29-30 NLT

God was on a mission to set righteousness back into focus. He knew that the only way things were going to improve was if He stepped in—all His other candidates had stepped back.

You might think your response would have been different. Perhaps you believe you would have been a man of courage who unwaveringly followed God's leading.

That's easier said than done.

Stepping up to follow God means experiencing a lot of "what ifs" and "how abouts." It means intentionally walking away from who you've been and moving toward wherever God is. Stepping up doesn't come naturally: it takes active engagement in training and a willingness to lead others just as you are led by God.

As a Christian, you must realize that standing in the gap is part of your job description—waiting fearfully in the crowd was never an option. You were designed to be courageous. But a man of courage will never succeed if he thinks his courage is found in himself.

Your feet were meant to walk with God.

How have you attempted to stand in the gap in the past? What can you do today to help God rebuild your culture's wall of righteousness?

Be the Man
WHO STEPS OUT

Then flew one of the seraphims unto me, having a live coal in his hand, which he had taken with the tongs from off the altar: And he laid it upon my mouth, and said, Lo, this hath touched thy lips; and thine iniquity is taken away, and thy sin purged. And I heard the voice of the Lord, saying, Whom shall I send, and who will go for us? Then said I, Here am I; send me.

ISAIAH 6:6-8 KJV

David Livingstone was a gifted author, explorer, and missionary to Africa. If that sounds like an impressive resume, you should know Livingston was more willing than he was prepared. He failed his missionary exam and would have been rejected had the missionary board not agreed to give him a rare second chance.

Stepping out of your comfort zone requires a powerful resolve and a deep sense of courage—and that's just the kind of courage the prophet Isaiah had. When God asked for volunteers, Isaiah bravely responded, "I'm right here. I'm willing to go. You can send me."

His journey wasn't easy. While God insisted on leading

the people, the people insisted on running away. When God asked them to follow, they played a high-stakes game of hide and seek. But through it all, Isaiah remained faithful to his calling.

This same God who discovered willingness in Isaiah and David Livingstone is asking today, "Whom shall I send?" Often, it's easier to look around and wonder who's going to answer. But have you ever considered that God might be asking *you*?

God is waiting for you to listen, raise your hand, and shout, "I'm right here. I'm willing to go. You can send me."

When was the last time God gave you an opportunity to step out? How did you respond? How can you be more courageous in stepping out to follow God's directions?

Be the Man
WHO LIVES BY FAITH

Now the one who has fashioned us for this very purpose is God, who has given us the Spirit as a deposit, guaranteeing what is to come. Therefore we are always confident and know that as long as we are at home in the body we are away from the Lord. We live by faith, not by sight.

2 CORINTHIANS 5:5–7 NIV

In the vicinity of Oregon's Multnomah Falls, faith was on display as a woman dangled over a drop of three hundred feet. The only thing standing between her and doom was a well-placed tree root, which she strongly grasped. Her arms were tiring, and she could find no foothold. She *had* to believe the root would hold—the only other option was unacceptable.

This woman had no guarantee that someone would find her or even be able to help. But as she held on, hope kept her vision of rescue alive.

What a profound picture of your faith in God! As you cling to the root of God's Word, God promises that rescue is coming. He will step in and lift you up, allowing you to share your story with others at the end of your struggle.

"But why," you might ask, "doesn't God let me see into the future?" The answer is simple: if you knew every detail of every experience you'll ever face, then the joy of the journey would be diminished. With nothing left to surprise you, why would you need courage?

It takes a man of courage to believe God's promises when there's no strength left to hang on. Faith doesn't need to know what's next—it just knows who's coming to your rescue.

How does the Spirit's presence in your life transform your decision making and help you write a new chapter in your story today?

Be the Man
WHO STANDS STRONG

It was by faith that Noah built a large boat to save his family from the flood. He obeyed God, who warned him about things that had never happened before. By his faith Noah condemned the rest of the world, and he received the righteousness that comes by faith.

HEBREWS 11:7 NLT

Imagine the curiosity that Noah's neighbors must have felt as they watched him and his family build a massive boat on dry land. And imagine their even greater bewilderment once animals began to arrive!

This project took more than a hundred years to complete. Day after day, Noah and his sons took hammers in hand, knowing their neighbors didn't understand what they were doing or why. The Bible doesn't say that Noah was mocked, but it's hard to imagine any other response. The people probably couldn't help tossing in some choice bits of mockery and sarcasm.

Noah had never piloted an ocean vessel before, and he probably wasn't even a carpenter. But it was God who drew up the plans. . .all Noah had to do was obey. For more than a century, this man stood strong. He probably had days in which he wanted to quit, but God's command was clear—and He never suggested that Noah could stop.

God took a story whose end was unknown and combined it with an adventure no one had ever experienced. But this seemingly outlandish plan saved the lives of Noah, his wife, his sons, and a floating zoo.

You can experience the same discovery at the place where God's plan and your purpose collide. Even when people don't understand your need to follow God, all you must do is stand strong.

Is anything preventing you from standing unashamed as a Christian? How does Noah's story inspire you to keep following God?

Be the Man
WHO MOVES FORWARD

Thus saith the LORD, which maketh a way in the sea, and a path in the mighty waters; Which bringeth forth the chariot and horse, the army and the power; they shall lie down together, they shall not rise: they are extinct, they are quenched as tow. Remember ye not the former things, neither consider the things of old. Behold, I will do a new thing; now it shall spring forth; shall ye not know it?

ISAIAH 43:16–19 KJV

Plenty of movies involve someone whose good, problem-free life is torn apart by a worst-case scenario. The rest of the movie often features the protagonist overcoming roadblocks on his quest to get back to the good old days.

God, however, doesn't think this way. His map for your life doesn't loop back to the place right before your failure; instead, it stretches onward, using that failure as a springboard to reach even greater heights than before.

God's plan for your life requires courage. After all, complacency is much easier than adventure. That's why some people stick with their jobs, even when better opportunities present themselves. There is security in what is familiar.

But God, in a burst of superior wisdom, has forged a way through the ordinary, and the destination is amazing! The road will be rough, and you might sometimes think you've taken a harder path. But when you trust God and move forward, you'll look back one day, convinced He led you to a better place.

Your story isn't a movie, so trading your new life for old habits will always be unwise. Getting started may be the hardest—but most important—step you take.

Do you ever struggle with embracing your new life over the old? If so, what will it take to adjust your vision toward the goal?

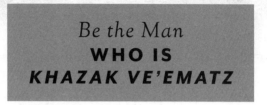

Be the Man
WHO IS
KHAZAK VE'EMATZ

"Be strong and very courageous. Be careful to obey all the law my servant Moses gave you; do not turn from it to the right or to the left, that you may be successful wherever you go. Keep this Book of the Law always on your lips; meditate on it day and night, so that you may be careful to do everything written in it. Then you will be prosperous and successful. Have I not commanded you? Be strong and courageous. Do not be afraid; do not be discouraged, for the LORD your God will be with you wherever you go."

JOSHUA 1:7-9 NIV

In the Hebrew language, the English words *strong* and *courageous* are spoken as *khazak ve'ematz.*

Whenever a Hebrew heard these words, that person would likely automatically think of Joshua's story. When Joshua took Moses' place in leading the people into the promised land, he was undoubtedly intimidated. After all, not even Moses—whom God used to set the people free—could get the people to the land God had given them. How could Joshua have expected to succeed where such a noble man had failed?

That's when God commanded Joshua to *khazak ve'ematz*—be strong and courageous. God gave this command more than once, driving home the point that neither fear nor discouragement was welcome. God, who could do the impossible, was with him.

Today, exercise your faith and choose to follow God. It doesn't matter what language you speak or what dialect you understand—the concept behind the words *strong* and *courageous* is universal.

The God with whom you walk is bigger than any obstacle that stands in your way.

Do fear and discouragement ever hinder your walk with God? If so, how can you work on being stronger and more courageous?

Be the Man
WHO HUMBLY RESISTS

Do you think the Scriptures have no meaning? They say that God is passionate that the spirit he has placed within us should be faithful to him. And he gives grace generously. As the Scriptures say, "God opposes the proud but gives grace to the humble." Humble yourselves before God. Resist the devil, and he will flee from you.

JAMES 4:5–7 NLT

Motivation plays a huge role in your life story. It's the very thing that gives you the desire to become a man of courage—without it, you'll be stuck cowering in a corner, incapable of following God's positive change.

In order to be humble before God, you must be motivated to see God as bigger, wiser, and bolder than you are. And in order to resist the devil, you must be motivated to follow God.

The problem for most men is that when the devil makes his debut, they blindly accept his invitation. The devil doesn't want you to seek God, so he'll make fun of you for thinking you need Him. And once Satan convinces you that you don't need God or that God is withholding good things from you, that's when he has you right where he wants you. To resist his influence, you must believe that the enemy's words, though they sound like silk, are actually filled with venom.

Thankfully, God's resources can motivate you to resist. And whenever that happens, the devil gets really uncomfortable. He can't stay long when God is welcome.

Whatever you believe deep down is what determines the direction you'll go. . .and who you'll follow to get there.

Do you have a strong motivation to follow God and resist the devil? If so, how is this motivation evidenced in your life?

Be the Man
WHO DOES SOMETHING

Only be thou strong and very courageous, that thou mayest observe to do according to all the law, which Moses my servant commanded thee: turn not from it to the right hand or to the left, that thou mayest prosper withersoever thou goest. This book of the law shall not depart out of thy mouth; but thou shalt meditate therein day and night, that thou mayest observe to do according to all that is written therein: for then thou shalt make thy way prosperous, and then thou shalt have good success.

JOSHUA 1:7–8 KJV

It's been said that meditation is the art of doing nothing. But what if meditation instead means filling your mind and spirit with so much good news that the lingering bits of nothing get washed away?

If time is of the essence, then engaging in worthless pursuits doesn't make sense. The meditation that God describes may be more aptly compared to a jeweler who examines a diamond through a magnifying lens. Whenever you search for brilliance and clarity in God's Word, dwelling on it in the process, you will replenish your appreciation for God. That way, you'll have something to believe in rather than nothing worth talking about.

When you know what God says and understand what He wants, you won't miss what He wishes for you to learn and do. Also, by closely reading a scripture passage—as well as the verses around it for context—you leave with a gem that can impact your understanding of God's truth.

Meditate when you wake up, when you make your morning commute, and when you struggle to sleep at night—your spiritual success may well depend on it.

Do you ever think meditation is a waste of time? If so, how can you turn it into the art of doing something?

Be the Man
WHO CAPTURES THOUGHTS

I beg you that when I come I may not have to be as bold as I expect to be toward some people who think that we live by the standards of this world. For though we live in the world, we do not wage war as the world does. The weapons we fight with are not the weapons of the world. On the contrary, they have divine power to demolish strongholds. We demolish arguments and every pretension that sets itself up against the knowledge of God, and we take captive every thought to make it obedient to Christ.

2 Corinthians 10:2-5 niv

There is something appealing to men about the life of a warrior. Warriors are brave men of valor, and their lives represent purpose and adventure. They are aligned with a cause, and they have a leader to follow.

You are called to be a "word warrior." This war isn't physical, and it doesn't involve vanquishing those who hold different opinions. Rather, it involves compassionately challenging bad ideas with God's truth.

This battle starts by challenging your own thinking.

It will be hard to convince anyone of God's truth if you don't believe it (or know it) yourself. Therefore, take your own thoughts captive, interrogate each one, and contrast them with what God actually said. Don't settle for secondhand accounts. Your belief should come from a personal knowledge of God's Word.

God's enemy will try to challenge your convictions, setting up shop in your mind and disputing each truth you interrogate. He will be an advocate for the status quo. He is pleased whenever there's a mismatch between what you think and what God says.

Don't let the enemy stop you from entering truth's doors—be the warrior that God calls you to be today.

Do you have any thoughts that contradict God's Word? If so, how can you challenge them?

Be the Man
WHO SEES HIMSELF CLEARLY

"Why worry about a speck in your friend's eye when you have a log in your own? How can you think of saying to your friend, 'Let me help you get rid of that speck in your eye,' when you can't see past the log in your own eye? Hypocrite! First get rid of the log in your own eye; then you will see well enough to deal with the speck in your friend's eye."

MATTHEW 7:3–5 NLT

At some point, someone will say something that you know is not true. Many trustworthy people might believe the lie and pass it on as solid intel. Consequently, misinformation will be accepted without challenge.

When you recognize a falsehood, you might be tempted to jump up, shout the person down, and tell everyone the truth. If you do, however, most people will be more inclined to remember your awkward outburst than they will the lie. Your own fault will have overshadowed the fault you sought to correct.

Jesus' metaphor of the log and speck has everything to do with perspective. If you have a large object in your eye, your window of vision shrinks dramatically, altering your perception of the world around you.

Similarly, when you have a big sin in your life, you should be able to notice it. But instead, it creates a blind spot when it comes to your own sin and amplifies whatever tiny sins you spot in others.

Confronting your own sin takes humility and courage. But it will not only improve your own spiritual eyesight— it will also make you compassionate when dealing with the sin you see in others.

Do you spend time working on your own spiritual vision? How compassionate are you when it comes to the sins of others?

Be the Man
WHO HAS A LONG VIEW

For which cause we faint not; but though our outward man perish, yet the inward man is renewed day by day. Our light affliction, which is but for a moment, worketh for us a far more exceeding and eternal weight of glory; While we look not at the things which are seen, but at the things which are not seen: for the things which are seen are temporal; but the things which are not seen are eternal.

2 CORINTHIANS 4:16-18 KJV

If you tell a struggling friend, "Don't worry. You'll get over it," you may technically be right, but you might have to look for a new friend. Most people don't take kindly to such platitudes.

Yet when God expresses this sentiment, it's not a platitude. He doesn't criticize the hurt He sees in others but instead compassionately reminds them that their struggles won't last forever. Bad times will come to an end. In the eye of the storm, it's hard to see what God is doing, but this temporary pain will provide an unimaginable payoff.

God is the absolute best at transforming worst-case

scenarios into exceptional outcomes. He can make scars beautiful. Restoration is possible to those who are broken, battered, and forgotten.

Courageous men understand that eternity is forever, so the relatively short lifespan we live here means very little compared to all the good that is yet to come for us who love God and live for His kingdom.

So take a long view. Remember that whatever you face will not be faced forever, and your reward can never be invaded by trouble. You live a short time here. . .but forever with God.

Do you sometimes find it hard to remember that trouble is a short-term issue? How can you remind yourself that bad days will never last?

Be the Man
WHO DISCOVERS STRENGTH

I can do all this through him who gives me strength.

PHILIPPIANS 4:13 NIV

Many verses need a little context to understand them. Philippians 4:13 is no exception.

Often, people gain comfort through a surface level reading of this verse. They believe that God will give them the strength to do *anything*—that there's nothing they can't accomplish. But what happens if you factor in the previous verse? Philippians 4:12 says, "I know what it is to be in need, and I know what it is to have plenty. I have learned the secret of being content in any and every situation, whether well fed or hungry, whether living in plenty or in want" (NIV).

Clearly, Paul didn't mean you can dream up anything you want and God has to give it to you. God does want you to dream big, but He never offers a blank check. Rather, Paul's words came from a specific place of courageous wonder.

Sometimes, the apostle ate well; at other times, he

went hungry. There were good days and days that seemed doomed from the start. However, instead of complaining to customer support whenever he encountered some supply chain issues, Paul simply said, "I can do all this through him who gives me strength."

He recognized that no one is wired to get through hard days alone—God's help is required. So during these bad times, God's comfort was imperative. His compassion was Paul's rock of refuge, which reminded him that God's dream was worth following and that His ultimate plan dwarfs even the most wonderful of days.

Do you sometimes complain when you don't get exactly what you want? If so, how can you learn to lean more fully on God's comfort and help?

Be the Man
WHO IS AN ESSENTIAL ANALYST

If there be therefore any consolation in Christ, if any comfort of love, if any fellowship of the Spirit, if any bowels and mercies, Fulfil ye my joy, that ye be likeminded, having the same love, being of one accord, of one mind. Let nothing be done through strife or vainglory; but in lowliness of mind let each esteem other better than themselves. Look not every man on his own things, but every man also on the things of others.

PHILIPPIANS 2:1-4 KJV

Computers can seem a lot like human intellect—that's because human intellect developed them. They analyze data and compute a response. The better the data, the better the analysis. These devices aren't prone to snap judgements, prejudice, or personal preference. They only respond to data and not what motivated the data.

God wants you to be one of His analysts. Whenever you see that someone has a need, pray to God, and He will help you calculate how to respond.

It's often easy to let your personal desires control

your response as you ignore any certain data associated with the needs of others. God, however, has an essential analyst update—His Spirit—that allows you to take this extra data into account and respond with empathy and compassion. Some people can't seem to be courageous in helping because they haven't accessed this essential upgrade.

You are more than a computer—you are flesh and bone analyzing flesh and bone, so what you discover will be more than hard facts and bottom lines. Being an essential analyst brings you to a place of connection with those you are learning to care about.

How good are you at analyzing the needs of others? What can you do to extend kindness to those who need help?

Be the Man
WHO SHARES THE LOAD

Share each other's burdens, and in this way obey the law of Christ.

GALATIANS 6:2 NLT

Golfers hire a caddy when they want someone else to carry their clubs. People hire moving companies when they need their belongings moved from one location to the next. A family might hire someone to do some light housekeeping or care for an aging family member or young child whenever the need arises. All these are examples of people who share another's burdens—yet only when they're asked.

What about when nobody asks but you know it's the right thing to do?

Take eleven-year-old Davyon, for instance. He has always wanted to become an emergency medical technician when he grows up. Apparently, he just couldn't wait. One day at lunch, he came to the rescue of a choking student and helped dislodge the food. Later the same day, he helped rescue a neighbor from a burning house.

Davyon is an example of someone who kept his eyes peeled for ways to help share another person's burden. In his case, he also saved two lives.

Have you made a habit out of stepping up to share someone's load? Being a Christian doesn't mean you'll never have time for yourself—it simply means widening the scope of your interests to include others.

Selfishness refuses to include others and laments every occasion when one's personal time and space is breached. But God asks for a different response. His love is for all people everywhere, and He's in the business of saving lives and transforming hearts. Because He shares your burdens, He asks you to do the same.

Relationships are just that important to Him.

How has someone else shared a burden you faced? How has God? What might motivate you to share someone else's burden?

Be the Man
WHO WALKS THE EXTRA MILE

"If anyone wants to sue you and take your shirt, hand over your coat as well. If anyone forces you to go one mile, go with them two miles. Give to the one who asks you, and do not turn away from the one who wants to borrow from you."

MATTHEW 5:40-42 NIV

In a more distant past, it was normal to conscript someone into forced labor. *Conscription* means the compulsory enlistment for a service to be performed. More recently, this word was used to describe the draft that brought young soldiers into the armed forces. Both meanings suggest involuntary service.

Jesus knew this kind of service was a normal part of life in His culture. Therefore, He told His disciples that if they found themselves forced to help someone, they shouldn't stop at the bare minimum. Rather, they should set the bar much higher and do even more than they were asked. This response didn't stem from a desire for recognition. It proved they were Christians who represented God. After all, if they were to treat others as if they were accommodating God Himself, then why would it matter if anyone was paying attention?

Think about what your life would be like if God behaved like we do sometimes. Would He say, "Sorry, I can't help you right now. I'm on the clock"?

Never! That's just not who He is.

Other people's needs will never be met if you lack empathy. God tells us that we should go above and beyond to help others. After all, isn't that what He did for us?

When you answer someone's call for help, do you go beyond what's needed or stop once the minimum is reached? How does God's example help you see the right response?

Be the Man
WHO PERFORMS ACTS OF KINDNESS

We know what real love is because Jesus gave up his life for us. So we also ought to give up our lives for our brothers and sisters. If someone has enough money to live well and sees a brother or sister in need but shows no compassion—how can God's love be in that person? Dear children, let's not merely say that we love each other; let us show the truth by our actions.

1 JOHN 3:16–18 NLT

A man's courage is never stronger than when he's doing something that defies expectation. If greed is the common response, then a courageous man shows generosity. He may experience ridicule, but he also understands that God has a different set of rules for His family. If following those rules makes him seem peculiar, then so be it.

Kindness rarely makes the headlines, but it's constantly impacting families around the world. Some churches have even tried increasing acts of kindness by giving their members money and asking them to use it exclusively for others. These churches hope that this investment will help their congregation experience firsthand the joy that intentional acts of kindness bring. Many members will return with stories about what God did when they used their gift.

Kindness can be a good way for you to show God's selfless, heart-changing love to people who doubt it exists. Actions like walking someone's dog, generously tipping a waiter, or paying for a stranger's meal may be small, but they make a very visible point. When others see it, maybe they will also see the God who inspired it.

When was the last time you saw kindness make a positive impact? Why did that happen? Do others see God's love in your own kindness?

Be the Man
WHO IS LION-BOLD

The wicked flee when no man pursueth: but the righteous are bold as a lion.

PROVERBS 28:1 KJV

Darkness falls and evil makes its way to the heart of our world. That's not the tagline for a new movie—it's a simple truth that the Bible addresses repeatedly. Jesus said, "Light is come into the world, and men loved darkness rather than light, because their deeds were evil" (John 3:19 KJV). The apostle Paul urged Christians in Rome, "let us therefore cast off the works of darkness, and let us put on the armour of light" (Romans 13:12 KJV).

When people do the wrong thing, they often try to hide it. Whenever they choose to sin, they want to conceal any evidence in the darkest part of their hearts.

People who sin don't want to get caught. They seal their lips, close their heart, and distance themselves from people who care about them. They run when no one chases and live in constant fear of being exposed. They believe their life will be destroyed if they're caught, so they cower in terror.

On the opposite end of the spectrum is the courageous man. His inscription reads, "Bold as a lion." This description doesn't refer to pride, but to truth. He knows that the path to forgiveness lies in God's embrace, so he freely runs toward it.

The brave, strong, and courageous are bold like lions simply because God has rescued them from the darkness and brightened them with His love.

How "lionlike" are you today?

Have you abandoned darkness in favor of light?
How can you learn to be more lion-bold?

Be the Man
WHO LIVES WITHOUT FEAR

Remember those in prison, as if you were there yourself. Remember also those being mistreated, as if you felt their pain in your own bodies. . . . God has said, "I will never fail you. I will never abandon you." We can say with confidence, "The LORD is my helper, so I will have no fear. What can mere people do to me?"

HEBREWS 13:3, 5–6 NLT

Imagine yourself as a six-year-old boy with a loving teenage brother. You think of him as your protector and defender. There's no reason to be afraid when someone bigger and stronger, with much more authority, is watching out for you. "Big brother" can keep the bullies away, make decisions you don't know how to make, and offer companionship when you really need a friend. Hopefully, he's always available when you need him.

It's nice to have help when bad things happen, but there is no better help than that which comes from the God who made you. When life's bullies show up, you can say, "When you mess with me you mess with *Him*."

That might cause bullies to reconsider their plans.

Men of courage are convinced that no one will ever exceed God's strength, cause Him to back down, or have a more authoritative name. They know that God's presence ensures a positive outcome.

You can be courageous under pressure when you remind yourself, "God helps me and I'm not afraid. People can never hurt me more than God loves me!"

What frightens you more than anything else? How can remind yourself that God is bigger than even your worst scenario?

Be the Man
WHO HAS ASTONISHING UNDERSTANDING

When they saw the courage of Peter and John and realized that they were unschooled, ordinary men, they were astonished and they took note that these men had been with Jesus.

ACTS 4:13 NIV

Dan had a background in broadcasting and a lifelong friendship with Jesus. So when a congregation needed a sermon for the weekend, they asked him to preach. Without a formal education, Dan stepped behind the pulpit, drew a deep breath, and began speaking about things he felt certain God had been teaching him. He enjoyed the experience. When he was asked again, it was easier to say yes. Eventually, Dan became the pastor of a small church. It wasn't a full-time job, and he had no formal degree, but he served with an equal blend of passion and perseverance. He embraced this role until he died.

Dan followed in the footsteps of Peter and John. It's easy to forget that these disciples weren't traditional religious leaders—even the people who heard them speak struggled to believe it. After all, the duo spoke as men who knew what they were talking about!

Yet these men were just ordinary fishermen until Jesus asked them to do something new. Courage allowed them to follow the call.

You can be courageous in sharing what you know with your family, friends, and coworkers. God didn't lock His saving grace behind a wall of education. You don't need a few letters after your name to share His story. Like Dan, Peter, and John, you have opportunities every day to share good news, no matter what you do for a living.

Have you ever backed down from telling people about God because you thought you lacked the right education? Have you devoted yourself to lifelong learning at Jesus' feet?

Be the Man
WHO SEEKS AUDIENCE WITH GOD

For we have not an high priest which cannot be touched with the feeling of our infirmities; but was in all points tempted like as we are, yet without sin. Let us therefore come boldly unto the throne of grace, that we may obtain mercy, and find grace to help in time of need.

HEBREWS 4:15-16 KJV

The boss sits in his office, reviewing paperwork and rubbing his temples. A sigh occasionally escapes his lips, and displeasure is etched across his face.

Would this be a good time to step into his office to ask for a raise?

Maybe not. Instead, you read the room, choosing to keep your head down and avoid disrupting your boss at all costs. Maybe you'll ask some other time.

Many people refuse to pray because this is how they view God. *It's a bad time to talk*, they think. *He's got too much on His plate right now. He'll get upset if I bug Him.*

But God isn't like that. He doesn't worry, and nothing

surprises Him. He doesn't have to contemplate business strategies or the latest news. He can pay full attention to whomever is courageous enough to get in touch. There is no bad time to pray, no hurt that can't be discussed, and no concern that will bother God. He's given you the right to consult with Him at any time about anything. He brings a listening ear to the table and then adds His mercy and grace. They are all yours.

So today, step up, speak out, and stand strong, seeking God's help when you need it most. There is no reason to delay. You have His permission.

Pray.

How similar to your boss is your idea of God?
Do you feel courageous when seeking His help?

Be the Man
WHO ACCEPTS STRENGTH

I give you thanks, O LORD, with all my heart; I will sing your praises before the gods. I bow before your holy Temple as I worship. I praise your name for your unfailing love and faithfulness; for your promises are backed by all the honor of your name. As soon as I pray, you answer me; you encourage me by giving me strength.

PSALM 138:1–3 NLT

Courage is not generally required when you only do the things you want to do. If you want to say something rude to someone, there's probably no need to access courage. When choosing to buy something you want, you simply pull it off the shelf and pay for it.

If these personal choices come naturally, then why do we need courage? You need courage whenever you're embracing the change that God brings to your heart. God has a new direction for you, and it takes courage to "walk in newness of life" (Romans 6:4 KJV).

A man of courage knows he is on a mission. His quest began the day he was brave enough to believe that God was more than a child's bedtime story. This adventure he's on requires courage, and the strength found in that courage is his for the asking.

Discouragement is far easier to accept, however, especially when you're challenged to rise above the average and do something special for God. That's why God's encouragement is so important—it helps you fulfill your purpose with passion and endurance.

God offers strength, so it just makes sense to accept it. He answers prayer, so you should pray. God can and will finish what He started, so be courageous and let Him complete the work He wants to do in your life.

Have you accepted God's strength to complete your quest? How can His courage inspire you to rise above what's "normal"?

Be the Man
WHO DOESN'T JUST WATCH

Be on your guard; stand firm in the faith; be courageous; be strong.

1 CORINTHIANS 16:13 NIV

When you watch a sporting event on television, what do you see in the stands? You undoubtedly spot numbered jerseys, foam fingers, and special headgear—whether corn cobs or cheese wedges or dawg masks. If you could visit those fans' homes, you'd probably find logo cups, pennants, or even a game-worn jersey or pair of socks in a frame. Real fans take pride in living vicariously through the actions of players they've likely never met.

But there's a much more important game—the game of life—that beckons you. God is inviting you to step away from the sidelines and engage in the rough and tumble of the actual contest. You'll need more courage and strength than you can summon on your own, so expect your great coach's assistance. You won't just be a fan—you'll be out on the field, embracing the quest with these instructions in mind:

1. Be on your guard: opposition is coming, so keep your eyes peeled and have your response ready.
2. Stand firm in the faith: believe that God has already won the victory.
3. Be courageous: fear has no place on this field.
4. Be strong: your coach will transform your weakness into the strength you need.

You can't be a Christian and just watch from the sidelines. There's a playbook to be studied. There's work to be done. There are teammates to support and encourage. Go get into the game!

Which of the four game instructions is the hardest for you? What is your motivation to follow God's playbook?

Be the Man
WHO HELPS
RESTORE COURAGE

Paul said unto Barnabas, Let us go again and visit our brethren in every city where we have preached the word of the Lord, and see how they do. And Barnabas determined to take with them John, whose surname was Mark. But Paul thought not good to take him with them, who departed from them from Pamphylia, and went not with them to the work.

Acts 15:36–38 KJV

A recurring storyline in police procedurals finds a well-respected officer nursing bitterness toward a partner due to a betrayal. The veteran officer never wants to work with that partner again, but they are predictably forced back together through a very specific set of circumstances. The betraying officer, we learn, was either misunderstood or has grown up since they last worked together, and the rest of the movie (and usually the sequel) functions as a buddy cop drama.

A similar plot ran deep in the missionary world of the apostle Paul and his friend Barnabas. They were the veterans of the early missionary program, and several rookies were advancing through the ranks. Then there was John Mark, who betrayed the veterans by leaving before the work was done. No note. No apology. No postcard from home.

You can probably understand why Paul was not especially thrilled when Barnabas proposed bringing John Mark back!

But Barnabas showed courage in brokering the return, Paul showed courage in eventually accepting him back, and John Mark showed courage in coming back—despite the intense awkwardness he knew would follow. In the end, Paul instructed Timothy, "Take Mark, and bring him with thee: for he is profitable to me for the ministry" (2 Timothy 4:11 KJV). God's restoration doesn't leave the willing behind.

Are you still reeling from a shocking and hurtful betrayal? If so, how might you offer forgiveness to that person today?

Be the Man
WHO KNOWS THE OVERCOMER

Jesus asked, "Do you finally believe? But the time is coming—indeed it's here now—when you will be scattered, each one going his own way, leaving me alone. Yet I am not alone because the Father is with me. I have told you all this so that you may have peace in me. Here on earth you will have many trials and sorrows. But take heart, because I have overcome the world."

JOHN 16:31-33 NLT

Life is filled with good news and bad news—and sometimes, they can both rush in all at once. You welcome the good and wish the bad would take a vacation. So far, however, it hasn't booked a trip.

Jesus spoke the truth in love, and He sugarcoated nothing. He gave some bad news first: the disciples would never escape trouble and sadness. But then the good news: this trouble didn't need to affect them. He never said He would overcome trouble in the future—no, Jesus said it was *already* overcome.

It's pretty clear that if trouble can't get the best of Jesus, then He's worth knowing, following, and obeying. You can allow this knowledge to change the way you think and strengthen you on your weak days. There's very little to be gained from wallowing in self-pity.

Yes, trouble is a common adversary to every man, but Jesus is an uncommon victor who can't be intimidated. Because you know the overcomer, you too can overcome. He did what no one else could so that you can be free from worry and fear. Someday, when you meet God in heaven, your trials and sorrow will become eternally past tense.

So today, feel free to choose the best response: courage.

Do you ever see your troubles as good news in disguise? Why is it important to acknowledge that trouble has been overcome?

Be the Man
WHO IGNORES
FOOLISH ADVICE

The serpent was more crafty than any of the wild animals the LORD God had made. He said to the woman, "Did God really say, 'You must not eat from any tree in the garden'?" The woman said to the serpent, "We may eat fruit from the trees in the garden, but God did say, 'You must not eat fruit from the tree that is in the middle of the garden, and you must not touch it, or you will die.'" "You will not certainly die," the serpent said to the woman.

GENESIS 3:1–4 NIV

You probably know a guy who has opinions on every subject you bring up. He's the armchair quarterback of wisdom. He has no real experience in the field or evidence to back up his claims, but that doesn't stop him from endlessly offering advice. You might even hesitate to bring up anything at all when he's around.

The serpent of Genesis is the first recorded example of a know-it-all. When the first woman told him what God had said, the serpent replied with an "Oh, really?"

He presented himself as an expert on the subject, and the woman believed his explanation over God's command.

Courage works to discard bad intel and accept direct orders. It chooses to believe truth and not some new, creative interpretation of the truth. It trusts God and rejects whatever contradicts Him. You are in connection with the God who really does know it all, so you don't have to be held hostage by the best guesses of other people.

Crafty speech will always twist the truth and lend credibility to unfounded theories. The serpent started the trend in a garden, and it's been growing ever since.

Will you be a disciple of deception, or will you know a lie when you see one?

Why is it sometimes easy to be deceived?
How can you show courage by seeking
the truth and then believing it?

Be the Man
WHO KNOWS HIS FATHER

Ye have not received the spirit of bondage again to fear; but ye have received the Spirit of adoption, whereby we cry, Abba, Father. The Spirit itself beareth witness with our spirit, that we are the children of God: And if children, then heirs; heirs of God, and joint-heirs with Christ; if so be that we suffer with him, that we may be also glorified together. For I reckon that the sufferings of this present time are not worthy to be compared with the glory which shall be revealed in us.

ROMANS 8:15–18 KJV

Have you ever noticed how fear is self-perpetuating? One fear indulged seems to circle back around with three or four more in tow. Before long, fear can become overwhelming and debilitating.

But if fear enslaves, then courage brings freedom. God's Spirit will always work with your spirit to eliminate worry even during alarming situations. Since you've accepted God's payment for the sin debt you owe, what could you possibly fear? Your past is forgiven. Your present is a work in progress. Your future is assured.

Because God is your Father, you have a change in status. You are an heir to the heaven He has created for His family. You are not a black sheep, a charity case, or a lost cause. God has released you from the bondage of fear, sin, and death. You have hope for a future without fear.

Courage understands that you exist in a temporary assignment and that there's more to this life than a dash on a tombstone. Each day, you have the chance to reject fear, follow courage, and embrace faith.

This is no fool's errand—it brings strength now and hope for eternity.

Do you sometimes give up God's blessings by holding on to fear? If so, how can you drop this fear and trust God is a good Father?

Be the Man
WHO LIKES REMINDERS

"When the Father sends the Advocate as my representative—that is, the Holy Spirit—he will teach you everything and will remind you of everything I have told you. I am leaving you with a gift—peace of mind and heart. And the peace I give is a gift the world cannot give. So don't be troubled or afraid."

JOHN 14:26–27 NLT

Teachers know how to teach. They share data and make sure to hit all the high points, reviewing their notes to ensure they don't skip anything that might show up on a test. They want to be both fair and thorough. Invariably, however, some of their words will refuse to stick to your cerebral cortex, and no matter how hard you try to retrieve the information, you'll keep drawing a blank.

The Christian man, however, gets both an instructor and a reminder whenever he needs it. Every test is open book.

The man of courage knows that each of God's reminders leads to answers. After all, repetition is vital in helping us remember what we're learning. Such a man, therefore, will refuse to argue when God's Spirit is guiding him through his test.

Today, you can tackle your trials confidently, knowing there's nothing you will face that God has not been preparing you for—and nothing that you'll ever need to endure alone. Somewhere beyond this trial, there's a reward for your passing grade.

So keep listening to the subtle promptings of God's Spirit. They contain life, hope, and purpose. They are yours to keep. . .and yours to share.

How often do you pay attention to what God's Spirit is teaching you? How does it inspire courage to know that God has chosen to develop His plan for you through His Spirit?

Be the Man
WHO CHOOSES TO BLESS

David gave his son Solomon the plans for the portico of the temple, its buildings, its storerooms, its upper parts, its inner rooms and the place of atonement. He gave him the plans of all that the Spirit had put in his mind for the courts of the temple of the LORD and all the surrounding rooms, for the treasuries of the temple of God and for the treasuries for the dedicated things. . . . David also said to Solomon his son, "Be strong and courageous, and do the work. Do not be afraid or discouraged, for the LORD God, my God, is with you. He will not fail you or forsake you until all the work for the service of the temple of the LORD is finished."

1 CHRONICLES 28:11-12, 20 NIV

In Jewish culture, it's normal for a father or grandfather to pass a blessing to his son or grandson. This act spoke life into the youth and gave them more defined possibilities for their lives. David, King of Israel, chose this method of blessing his son Solomon in this often-overlooked passage.

David, having been through challenge after challenge,

bore both heart wounds and battle scars. Yet this man, whenever he'd let his life wander, had made a habit of returning to God.

Solomon would be next in line. Therefore, David chose to equip his son with a blessing that carried three lessons:

1. Be strong and courageous: God had given him purpose and strength for his future.

2. Do not be afraid or discouraged: fear had no place in his actions.

3. God will not fail or forsake: even after David died, Solomon would receive instruction and advice from a King greater than his father.

David offered the blessing, Solomon was blessed, and God perfectly lived up to all that the new king could expect—and more!

What impact would a blessing like this have on your life? How can you use God's blessing to impact a new generation?

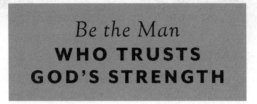

Be the Man
**WHO TRUSTS
GOD'S STRENGTH**

*The LORD is my light and my salvation; whom shall I fear?
the LORD is the strength of my life; of whom shall I be afraid?
When the wicked, even mine enemies and my foes, came upon
me to eat up my flesh, they stumbled and fell. Though an host
should encamp against me, my heart shall not fear: though war
should rise against me, in this will I be confident. One thing
have I desired of the LORD, that will I seek after; that I may
dwell in the house of the LORD all the days of my life, to behold
the beauty of the LORD, and to enquire in his temple.*

PSALM 27:1–4 KJV

A lot of things are out of your control—store prices,
unsafe drivers, unexpected home repairs, a medical diag-
nosis. The one thing you *can* control is how you respond.
Your response should be informed by the great gift giver,
whose commands encourage you to think differently
about your struggle.

Every day, the headlines tell stories of intimidation
and fear. There is always someone who wants you to

believe that you don't belong, you don't count, you can't win. God, however, doesn't want you to be afraid of bullies. He wants you to be courageous because His biggest strength is love. This love dispels fear wherever it's found.

God's light illuminates your path, so why would you be afraid? God's strength is greater than any mischief a person can devise—so why see anyone as an enemy? The man of courage is impressed by the God who dispels fear. Such men can make new choices and leave fear without a place at the table.

Have you ever feared someone who threatened or intimidated you? How can following God's directions lead you to send back any fear you may receive?

Be the Man
WHO KNOWS WHAT HE IS

See what great love the Father has lavished on us, that we should be called children of God! And that is what we are! The reason the world does not know us is that it did not know him. Dear friends, now we are children of God, and what we will be has not yet been made known. But we know that when Christ appears, we shall be like him, for we shall see him as he is.

1 JOHN 3:1–2 NIV

Many television movies are based on a tried-and-true formula: A boy meets a girl, and both try to convince themselves they are just friends. Suddenly, one of them realizes he or she has fallen in love—but then sees the other person talking to an old flame. In frustration, the disappointed lover leaves the scene, determined to forget the other person. But then events bring them back together again, and the movie ends in a sweet kiss.

God's love for you is different. No made-for-television plot could ever hope to capture it. He offers to make everyone His child, but each story will follow a different path.

God's love breaks down barriers of resistance and invites long conversations. This love paid for a priceless but necessary gift. God's love sent you an invitation and waited for you to accept.

When you do accept His love, Luke 15:10 says that "there is rejoicing in the presence of the angels of God" (NIV).

Knowing your identity will powerfully encourage your heart. Stand up, embrace confidence, and discover joy. You are God's redeemed and forgiven child, and He never misunderstands you. He won't rush out, even if it seems you are rejecting Him. You needed to be found, so He didn't stop until you were.

Now that's a great plot!

What part of God's redemptive story in your life makes you feel most grateful? How can God use your story to introduce Himself to others?

Be the Man
WHO FINDS COURAGE IN WAITING

Teach me how to live, O LORD. Lead me along the right path, for my enemies are waiting for me. Do not let me fall into their hands. For they accuse me of things I've never done; with every breath they threaten me with violence. Yet I am confident I will see the LORD's goodness while I am here in the land of the living. Wait patiently for the LORD. Be brave and courageous. Yes, wait patiently for the LORD.

PSALM 27:11–14 NLT

You've received good news: you're entitled to a tax refund! This news gives you a shot of boldness and confidence, and you immediately start formulating plans for what you will buy. But as the days go by and the refund doesn't appear, your confidence begins taking a back seat to fear. You find yourself refreshing your online bank page or taking one more look in your mail slot. Still? Nothing. How long must you wait?

It should come as no surprise that God often feels the need to remind you to wait for Him. His timing is very different from yours. He's not on the clock—He knows exactly when to show up with what you need.

Bold confidence comes with a unique blend of trust, patience, and a good memory. God has been good before, He is now, and He will be again. Don't spend any time trying to outthink Him—you'll never anticipate His next move. You may not see it when you take the first step or the hundredth, but just know that His move will be amazing.

Pay attention and keep waiting.

Have you ever felt like you've waited too long for God? Why is patience linked to courage?

Be the Man
WHO KNOWS WHEN NOT TO HESITATE

Because all those men which have seen my glory, and my miracles, which I did in Egypt and in the wilderness, and have tempted me now these ten times, and have not hearkened to my voice; Surely they shall not see the land which I sware unto their fathers, neither shall any of them that provoked me see it: But my servant Caleb, because he had another spirit with him, and hath followed me fully, him will I bring into the land whereinto he went; and his seed shall possess it.

NUMBERS 14:22–24 KJV

As a younger man, Caleb was part of a spying party Moses sent into the promised land. Ten of these twelve men returned with a report that the land's men were too big. The spies felt like grasshoppers in comparison. Consequently, most decided they should give up on the conquest and settle for wilderness living. Caleb and His friend Joshua, however, thought it was time to take the land that God had said was theirs.

The crowd sided with the doom-and-gloom brigade,

so God told the people they could hang out in the wilderness a few more years. Eventually, He would welcome Caleb and Joshua into the promised land, but the other ten wouldn't live to see that day.

Caleb was a man of courage—he believed that if God said the land was theirs, then not even giants could prevail against them.

He was right, of course. He had no good reason to doubt and every reason to trust, so he believed. Caleb would re-enter that land as an old man, settling it with a strength that remained just as potent as it was when he first laid eyes on the land.

Do you sometimes hesitate to take possession of what God says is yours? Does the knowledge that you have an adversary ever cause you to doubt if God can come through?

Be the Man
WHO UNDERSTANDS ASSURANCE

For those who are led by the Spirit of God are the children of God. The Spirit you received does not make you slaves, so that you live in fear again; rather, the Spirit you received brought about your adoption to sonship. And by him we cry, "Abba, Father." The Spirit himself testifies with our spirit that we are God's children. Now if we are children, then we are heirs—heirs of God and co-heirs with Christ, if indeed we share in his sufferings in order that we may also share in his glory.

ROMANS 8:14–17 NIV

You are not God's foster child. God doesn't just let you spend the day with Him and then make you go back to your old life. No, you are God's *child*.

Do you find this hard to believe? After all, this is God we're talking about. He's surely got more important things to do than spending time with you, right?

Wrong! The Bible says that even His Spirit tells you that You are His beloved child and that He'll never be too busy to listen to you.

God doesn't use your spiritual adoption papers to manipulate you either. So don't live with feelings of spiritual abandonment. These emotions are a lie from Satan. God does not leave or abandon, and He's promised great things to those who love Him.

This is assurance for the insecure, certainty for the doubter, and courage for the cowardly. God knew you before you were born (see Psalm 139:13)—you will never be an imposition to Him.

Does being assured of God's love enhance your courage? Has the adversary ever tried convincing you that God has abandoned you?

Be the Man
WHO IS UNASHAMED

Never be ashamed to tell others about our Lord. And don't be ashamed of me, either, even though I'm in prison for him. With the strength God gives you, be ready to suffer with me for the sake of the Good News. For God saved us and called us to live a holy life. He did this, not because we deserved it, but because that was his plan from before the beginning of time—to show us his grace through Christ Jesus. And now he has made all of this plain to us by the appearing of Christ Jesus, our Savior. He broke the power of death and illuminated the way to life and immortality through the Good News. And God chose me to be a preacher, an apostle, and a teacher of this Good News. That is why I am suffering here in prison. But I am not ashamed of it, for I know the one in whom I trust, and I am sure that he is able to guard what I have entrusted to him until the day of his return.

2 TIMOTHY 1:8-12 NLT

Paul was used to being in prison, and he never tried hiding from this part of his story. Why? He knew his story wasn't over yet.

Paul was convinced that beyond the dirt floor and bars, there was a God worth trusting. He had received a new life in Jesus, and God Himself was guarding this life. He was content knowing that even if he never saw the next sunrise, his eternal life with God was assured.

Don't give up or give in. Don't live in stress and fear. Never allow shame or guilt to prevent you from believing the truth: you serve a God who can break whatever prison bars may hold you.

If you're a Christian, condemnation has passed—you're now moving forward with God and will one day recognize that all your trials only brought you closer to the guardian.

Do you ever plan personal pity parties? If so, how can you learn to overcome this shame that damages your relationship with God?

Be the Man
WHO ACCEPTS A STRONG SONG OF SALVATION

I will trust, and not be afraid: for the LORD JEHOVAH is my strength and my song; he also is become my salvation. Therefore with joy shall ye draw water out of the wells of salvation. And in that day shall ye say, Praise the LORD, call upon his name, declare his doings among the people, make mention that his name is exalted. Sing unto the LORD; for he hath done excellent things: this is known in all the earth.

ISAIAH 12:2–5 KJV

Songs. They can be fun, serious, mournful, or wisely filled with worship. You may not pay attention to the words of worship music, choosing instead to focus on the soothing melody; however, the lyrics often beautifully proclaim God's perfection, taking our focus off our petty fears and onto divine, majestic truths.

Fear can keep you from honoring or even following God. Fear drains your spirit of strength. You can't hear God's song of salvation when anxiety is screaming in your soul. That's a horrible song to listen to, and it has no natural harmony.

But when you spend time with God, here's what He brings:

- Strength: You don't have it, but He does—and He'll give you all you need.
- Song: God inspires the words and melody that invite you to worship. His songs change you in ways that honor Him.
- Salvation: Without this, you would have neither strength nor a song. Salvation is God's plan to bring you away from the brink of spiritual death.

God's salvation, song, and strength are His gifts, and the courageous man accepts what He offers. So today, join His quest with enthusiasm. This is a life that begins and ends in the presence of God.

How can you draw closer to God through music? Do you frequently remind yourself that salvation is a gift only God can give?

Be the Man
WHO IS CRUSH RESISTANT

We have this treasure in jars of clay to show that this all-surpassing power is from God and not from us. We are hard pressed on every side, but not crushed; perplexed, but not in despair; persecuted, but not abandoned; struck down, but not destroyed. We always carry around in our body the death of Jesus, so that the life of Jesus may also be revealed in our body.

2 CORINTHIANS 4:7-10 NIV

Divers once called it "the bends." Today, the malady is more often referred to as "decompression sickness." It's a pressure issue that affects divers when they go underwater. When the human body takes in nitrogen gas from compressed air, this gas goes into the body tissue with potentially dangerous effects. If the diver ascends slowly, the nitrogen migrates to the lungs and gets expelled through normal breathing, but if the ascension is too rapid, bubbles of nitrogen form, remaining in the body and damaging nerves and tissue.

There are parallels here to the Christian life. Following Jesus should make us dramatically different from the people we were before. There are new pressures that seem bent on crushing us and thoughts that still float in our minds long after we've set them aside.

Escaping these pressures may seem like a perfect course of action, but they are really preparing you for your work in God's kingdom. If you try to rush away instead of allowing God to prepare you for your next assignment, you'll find yourself with a case of the spiritual "bends."

Just as coal under pressure becomes a diamond, so too can your life be transformed by life's pressure. God promises that no struggle needs to be final—and that no pressure needs to destroy you.

Can you recognize God's work through the pressures you've faced? How can these pressures lead you toward God's purpose?

Be the Man
WHO REMAINS CURIOUS

There was a man named Nicodemus, a Jewish religious leader who was a Pharisee. After dark one evening, he came to speak with Jesus. "Rabbi," he said, "we all know that God has sent you to teach us. Your miraculous signs are evidence that God is with you." Jesus replied, "I tell you the truth, unless you are born again, you cannot see the Kingdom of God." "What do you mean?" exclaimed Nicodemus. "How can an old man go back into his mother's womb and be born again?"

JOHN 3:1-4 NLT

Nicodemus knew a lot about God. He could tell you all the rules and how many times he'd obeyed them since breakfast. Nicodemus was used to seeing the Pharisees and religious leaders comparing their personal perfection, but he knew something was missing. He began to feel like he wasn't really living.

So Nicodemus took a courageous leap of faith by seeking Jesus out at night and asking Him to explain what He'd been teaching. He knew that if word got out about this secret meeting, he'd be both ridiculed and rejected by his own people. On the other hand, Nicodemus' curiosity had reached the boiling point, and the answers he received that night would alter his life forever.

As Jesus talked, understanding dawned in the mind of one who thought he knew it all. Suddenly, he became aware of the ineffectiveness of his old practices. And this courageous meeting climaxed with the greatest truth anyone had ever heard: "For this is how God loved the world: He gave his one and only Son, so that everyone who believes in him will not perish but have eternal life" (John 3:16 NLT).

Nicodemus met that Son, and you can meet Him too—every day.

Do you ever approach God with questions of your own? How does God use your curiosity to lead you to a place of courage?

Be the Man
WHO STOPS RUNNING TOWARD FEAR

We have known and believed the love that God hath to us. God is love; and he that dwelleth in love dwelleth in God, and God in him. Herein is our love made perfect, that we may have boldness in the day of judgment: because as he is, so are we in this world. There is no fear in love; but perfect love casteth out fear: because fear hath torment. He that feareth is not made perfect in love.

1 JOHN 4:16–18 KJV

Fear initiates a fight, flight, or freeze response, often producing a huge adrenaline rush. Fear struggles to sit still. It's erratic in its search for safety. But for the fearful, *nowhere* feels truly safe. Fear keeps you on the run, so the idea of putting down roots feels foreign and unacceptable.

On the other hand, love offers roots a chance to grow. Trust is welcome in this place, and courage finds a voice. Even if you experience a personal course correction, you'll never be rejected. When love moves in, fear is evicted. The two are not compatible.

A man of courage accepts God's love, refuses the adversary's fear, and allows his roots to grow deep into the new life that God offers.

Your life is a race, and love is leading you toward the finish line. You'll never be able to move toward God and recognize His love and acceptance if you're moving toward fear.

So what will you choose—cowardice or courage?

How much do you struggle with worry or fear?
How does love transform your relationship with God?

Be the Man
WHO KNOWS JESUS IS BIGGER THAN WHAT'S WRITTEN

Jesus performed many other signs in the presence of his disciples, which are not recorded in this book. But these are written that you may believe that Jesus is the Messiah, the Son of God, and that by believing you may have life in his name.

JOHN 20:30–31 NIV

There is always more to any story than a single person can share, but it's not always fruitful to try filling in the blanks. . .especially if the blank-filling contradicts what's already been established as truth.

The authors of the Gospels used personal observation and interviews to capture in print the things that Jesus did and taught. Some witnessed moments that others did not. No one wrote down *everything* about Jesus—that would be impossible. Yet what they did write was more than enough. Combined, their books form a love letter that clarifies the purpose of Jesus' arrival—you! The story of Jesus was written so that "you may believe that Jesus is the Messiah, the Son of God, and that by believing you may have life in his name."

Jesus brings new life to anyone who accepts His sacrifice. He didn't come to earth to do magic tricks. Nor did He come to demand His own desires and pleasure. Jesus came to rescue humanity, and He allowed enough of His story to be shared in order to show His purpose. Men of courage can say, "Count me in," as they study the written record of Jesus. . .and anticipate learning more in eternity.

What aspects of Jesus' story resonate the most with you? What comfort do you find in knowing that you were part of Jesus' purpose in coming to earth?

Be the Man
WHO'S A COURAGEOUS FRIEND

Jesus climbed into a boat and went back across the lake to his own town. Some people brought to him a paralyzed man on a mat. Seeing their faith, Jesus said to the paralyzed man, "Be encouraged, my child! Your sins are forgiven."... And the man jumped up and went home! Fear swept through the crowd as they saw this happen. And they praised God for giving humans such authority.

MATTHEW 9:1–2, 7–8 NLT

There was a healing in Israel, and Jesus was the healer. If there had been news media at the time, the story would've been front and center in the papers the next morning. Yet behind the sensational headline, there was another story too easy to ignore. Don't forget that a group of people had brought their paralyzed friend to Jesus.

Where's the story in that? This whole account is about the paralyzed man, right? Not entirely. Consider that the man's friends loved him enough to band together and try to bring him out of his dark desperation. They were bold enough to bring this man to Jesus, believing they would receive an answer.

Jesus actually performed two miracles that day: forgiving the man's sin and healing his body. Yet behind the miracles lay the courageous faith of friends. These individuals went the extra mile, confident that they had come to the right source. And Jesus met the paralyzed man's need on behalf of the faith of his friends.

You can be that kind of friend. You can carry your loved ones' pain to a God who can intervene in their lives—and loves to do so!

Do you believe God can do anything for your friends? If so, will you ask?

Be the Man
WHO BELIEVES IN A MIRACLE

Whom have I in heaven but thee? and there is none upon earth that I desire beside thee. My flesh and my heart faileth: but God is the strength of my heart, and my portion for ever.
PSALM 73:25–26 KJV

The low fuel light was blazing the entire drive to work, and the commuter didn't have a single penny left. There was no way to get the fuel needed to return home. The driver searched frantically under the car seats but found very little spare change. Suddenly, a gentleman working at the gas station knocked on the car window and told the driver that while he had no idea why, he had put a few dollars' worth of fuel on the pump for the customer. No charge. He hoped it helped.

Needless to say, the trip home was very emotional.

You live in a place where desperation lives. Circumstances leave you trembling, and you are certain that if God doesn't show up, you'll never make it through. But take heart: God is at work, and He brings to reality things that live above your wildest dreams. When He shows up in your life, the only word that can describe it is *miracle*.

Men of courage understand that any successful outcome comes from God's grace. Kids have broken toys, teens have broken hearts, and men sometimes struggle to hold on to the fragments of a broken life. But thankfully, God can take brokenness and work a restoration miracle.

Do you (or does someone you know) have a story of brokenness? When was the last time you asked God for help only He could provide?

Be the Man
WHO BELIEVES
BEYOND ALL ODDS

Some nations boast of their chariots and horses, but we boast in the name of the Lord our God. Those nations will fall down and collapse, but we will rise up and stand firm. Give victory to our king, O Lord! Answer our cry for help.

PSALM 20:7-9 NLT

Some men name their horses, some name their guns, some name their trucks. Some do all three. Men depend on these things and take great pride in them. They view any guy who thinks he has something superior as ridiculous and not worth a spare cup of coffee.

But as impressive as all this may be, God reminds you that His name, deeds, and attributes are far better. Because His faithfulness is beyond reproach, You can trust Him more than your most dependable horse, your most impressive truck, or your most powerful weapon.

At some point, all your earthly possessions will decay, break, or rust. The only thing that will survive is God, and He's been running the show for a *very* long time.

Faith takes courage. It means taking God at His word for things you've never witnessed. You didn't see the world created, but God says He did it. You didn't see Jesus die on the cross and rise again, but the Bible says it happened. Just as you don't doubt the Revolutionary War or the signing of the Declaration of Independence, though you weren't there for either one, you shouldn't doubt God's promises.

Trust the God who always exceeds your expectations. Believe. . .beyond all odds.

Do you sometimes trust your possessions or abilities over God? If so, how can you shift your trust away from the things you can see and toward the things you can't?

Be the Man
WHO FINISHES THE RACE

For I am already being poured out like a drink offering, and the time for my departure is near. I have fought the good fight, I have finished the race, I have kept the faith. Now there is in store for me the crown of righteousness, which the Lord, the righteous Judge, will award to me on that day—and not only to me, but also to all who have longed for his appearing.

2 TIMOTHY 4:6–8 NIV

Many men start the new year with vigor. They invest in a gym membership and tell themselves—and anyone willing to listen—that they'll be rising each morning before the crack of dawn, lifting weights until sweat breaks out, and buffing up so much that everyone will notice.

Then day two arrives. Suddenly, all motivation fades into a mirage, the body screams for relief, and any semblance of courage collapses into a small, discouraged whimper.

The pace God sets for your life is neither fast nor slow. It is, however, a relentless pursuit—a continual willingness to put one foot in front of the other. The satisfaction that comes at the end of this endurance race will be unmatched by any workout routine.

Fight hard, run well, and prove faithful. Show rare courage by asking God to show you the way. Ask Him, who knows that trouble is common, to also show compassion and give you determination on your journey.

Life isn't just about where you are in this moment—it's about where you find yourself at the end.

What are you doing today to help move you closer to God's finish line? Do you see following God's leadership as necessary for completing life's race?

Be the Man
WHO ISN'T SHAKEN

I know the LORD *is always with me. I will not be shaken, for he is right beside me.*

God was offering Moses an opportunity. He would deliver God's people from the oppression they'd endured at the hands of Pharaoh in Egypt. Moses, however, felt it was the perfect moment for full disclosure: he'd never done well in public speaking, he'd lived practically as a hermit for forty years, and. . .well. . .he was old. Moses was hunting for disqualification points, and he hoped his excuses were on point enough for God. *Surely*, he thought, *God has other, more qualified candidates!*

But Moses wasn't thinking about the people—he was thinking only about himself. Courage wasn't found in his response. His initial statement was essentially, "Not me! Not now!"

God gave His counteroffer in Exodus 3:12 (NLT): "I will be with you." What kind of argument can refute the help of the living God? Even with this perfect answer,

Moses still seemed interested in loopholes and excuses.

King David, who wrote today's scripture, had a different response to God. To this king, God wasn't unreasonable. If God requested him to follow, then God must know the way. Even more, he knew God would share all the tools he needed for the job.

God is right beside you, helping in ways you don't always understand. You could make excuses, but why? He can do so much more with your willingness instead. God has secured your future, and if He asks you to follow, then His plan cannot fail.

In God, you can refuse to be shaken.

How can your comfort zone negatively affect your willingness to obey God? Do you find it easier to make excuses than to believe God is right beside you?

Be the Man
WHO KNOWS GOD IS FOR US

What shall we then say to these things? If God be for us, who can be against us? He that spared not his own Son, but delivered him up for us all, how shall he not with him also freely give us all things? Who shall lay any thing to the charge of God's elect? It is God that justifieth.

ROMANS 8:31–33 KJV

The Philistines were a violent people prone to waging war and conquering lands. They seemed to think that if the giant Goliath was for them, then who could be against them? Day after day, the giant would call out and taunt the army of Israel.

Their tactic was working—no one wanted to fight them.

But these warriors got one crucial thing wrong: they put their trust in someone other than God. That meant their army was ripe for the picking.

When young David (the future king of Israel) walked onto the battlefield dressed like a shepherd, everyone laughed him to scorn. When he pulled out a sling and stone, nobody championed young David's cause. Yet David stuck to three undisputable facts: he was for God, God was with Him, and no one could stand against God. That day, the armies of Philistia and Israel witnessed just how big God is.

If you start believing that God is smaller than your problems, your thinking needs realigned. When you make anything bigger than God, you stand against the one who wants to stand for *you*.

With whom are you standing today?

How does this reminder of God's power challenge your fears? How will you live out your belief that God is bigger than anything you face?

Be the Man
WHO HAS WORTHY CONDUCT

Whatever happens, conduct yourselves in a manner worthy of the gospel of Christ. Then, whether I come and see you or only hear about you in my absence, I will know that you stand firm in the one Spirit, striving together as one for the faith of the gospel without being frightened in any way by those who oppose you. This is a sign to them that they will be destroyed, but that you will be saved—and that by God. For it has been granted to you on behalf of Christ not only to believe in him, but also to suffer for him, since you are going through the same struggle you saw I had, and now hear that I still have.

PHILIPPIANS 1:27–30 NIV

Paul had left the life of a religious leader to advocate for a relationship with Jesus, and he spent the rest of his life articulating the difference between the two. After planting a church in Philippi, he wanted to see spiritual growth in those who had chosen relationship over religion. The apostle often wondered if they would stand firm in their faith when he was absent. Would they be courageous representatives of the hope he had shared?

Paul's concern for the Christians in Philippi should remind us that faith is more than just an addition to our lives or a set of rules we follow—it's a friendship with God! This relationship changes your conduct, makes you crave fellowship with other Christians, and shines for everyone to see.

This is a call to a courageous, cooperative life. God wants to work in your life, but if you only follow another man's leading and refuse to listen to God's, then are you really a willing disciple?

Like Paul, those who introduced you to Jesus will want to hear that you follow God, even when they're out of town.

What's the difference between religion and relationship? Which one defines your life?

Be the Man
WHO GROWS THROUGH INSECURITY

"I know the LORD has given you this land," she told them. "We are all afraid of you. Everyone in the land is living in terror. For we have heard how the LORD made a dry path for you through the Red Sea when you left Egypt. And we know what you did to Sihon and Og, the two Amorite kings east of the Jordan River, whose people you completely destroyed. No wonder our hearts have melted in fear! No one has the courage to fight after hearing such things. For the LORD your God is the supreme God of the heavens above and the earth below."

JOSHUA 2:9–11 NLT

There is a whole lot of bluff in people who don't know God. Their insecurity shows up in false confidence. None of us know the future, but Christians know the God who does.

The Bible tells of two men who went to the walled city of Jericho. Joshua, having heard God's promise that the city would be overthrown, had sent these men to scout it out.

While in the city, a woman named Rahab recognized

that something new was happening and that the God of this advanced scouting team was supreme. So she sheltered the two men, knowing that if God wanted Jericho, nothing would stop Him. The only way of life she'd ever known was coming to a resounding end.

Although Rahab didn't know God, she had a willingness to admit her insecurity: "No wonder our hearts have melted in fear!" Rahab had little courage, but she had hope—hope that perhaps God would be gracious to her for not exposing the Hebrew scouting party.

Sometimes, courage begins with hope. Insecurity doesn't preclude you from the benefits of courage; instead, it could be the motivator that inspires you to let God fill in your gaps in knowledge, leading you to the life you've always needed.

When do you feel the most insecure?
How can you let God use this
insecurity to inspire courage?

Be the Man
WHO TRUSTS THE DEPENDABLE GOD

Be of good courage, and let us behave ourselves valiantly for our people, and for the cities of our God: and let the LORD do that which is good in his sight.

1 CHRONICLES 19:13 KJV

Joab thought like a warrior, acted like a warrior, and exuded the courage of a warrior in the face of any challenge. He worked to inspire his soldiers, and they fought hard for him. His warrior heart, however, must have been tinged with pride. Joab's strategies often replaced God's will. He often traded trust for deception. But one speech that he gave to his men seems to suggest that a kernel of truth remained lodged deep within his warring spirit.

Joab's words above presaged by centuries a quote attributed to Saint Ignatius: "Act as if everything depended on you; trust as if everything depended on God." Joab was very willing to go to war, but he concluded that in the end, God would do what God would do—even if Joab didn't like the outcome.

In the New Testament, another man was confronted with a similar struggle. He was a part of a group of religious leaders who had no use for the gospel. The group collectively sought to silence any talk about Jesus. But then this teacher, Gamaliel, said, "Let them alone: for if this counsel or this work be of men, it will come to nought: But if it be of God, ye cannot overthrow it" (Acts 5:38–39 KJV).

Men of courage know that their best plans may be in vain, but God's plans are always right. Be willing to set your plans aside when God reveals His better plan.

Have you ever refused to let God control your plans? If so, how did that turn out?

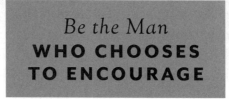

Be the Man
WHO CHOOSES
TO ENCOURAGE

Now I want you to know, brothers and sisters, that what has happened to me has actually served to advance the gospel. As a result, it has become clear throughout the whole palace guard and to everyone else that I am in chains for Christ. And because of my chains, most of the brothers and sisters have become confident in the Lord and dare all the more to proclaim the gospel without fear.

PHILIPPIANS 1:12–14 NIV

Madagascar is a great place, known for its wide variety of exotic creatures and an animated movie that bears its name. The island's past, however, was much darker.

In the mid 1800s, Christianity was outlawed in Madagascar. In the beginning of the purge, missionaries were targeted and made to leave. When Christianity didn't seem deterred, the queen resorted to confiscating land, forcing Christians into hard labor, and, finally, enacting the *tangena* ordeal. This "ordeal" involved the harvesting of a poisonous nut from the tangena tree and forcing a suspected Christian to consume it. Whoever lived through the experience was considered innocent; whoever died was declared guilty. It's been estimated that 20 percent of the total population died, but Christianity still continued to grow.

Sometimes, other Christians are emboldened by your struggles. It isn't that they want to see you struggle; rather, the example you set by trusting God encourages others to trust Him with their own struggles.

Be this kind of encourager.

Do you feel encouraged when you hear stories of brave Christian men who remained faithful? What part of your story could be an encouragement to others?

Be the Man
WHO UNDERSTANDS VICTORY

When our dying bodies have been transformed into bodies that will never die, this Scripture will be fulfilled: "Death is swallowed up in victory. O death, where is your victory? O death, where is your sting?" For sin is the sting that results in death, and the law gives sin its power. But thank God! He gives us victory over sin and death through our Lord Jesus Christ.

1 CORINTHIANS 15:54–57 NLT

You've probably heard the phrase, "Are you in it to win it?" This saying has a lot to unpack. If you really want to answer this question, a host of other questions arise. What are you in? Are you present? Are you engaged? Motivated? Do you believe your struggle is winnable? Do you need to do it all yourself, or will there be help? Is your opponent too big to conquer? What does *victory* mean? How will you know if you've won?

For the apostle Paul, his opponents were sin and death. Both separated men from God. But Paul clarified that God alone delivers victory. It wasn't by Paul's hard work, determination, or great personality.

You can never claim victory over sin and death alone. If you're it to win it, then make sure you bring Jesus with you. He's the one who orchestrated salvation—and He didn't need your help. In fact, God made it clear His standard is perfection, and you have nothing to offer (see Romans 3:23). This isn't a solo competition—you need God on your side if you ever hope to win.

God has always been in it to win it. Go with team God.

Do you ever struggle with the same sin repeatedly? Why is victory impossible when you try to go it alone?

Be the Man
WHO ISN'T JUST
BEHAVIOR MODIFIED

Finally, my brethren, be strong in the Lord, and in the power of his might. Put on the whole armour of God, that ye may be able to stand against the wiles of the devil. For we wrestle not against flesh and blood, but against principalities, against powers, against the rulers of the darkness of this world, against spiritual wickedness in high places. Wherefore take unto you the whole armour of God.

EPHESIANS 6:10–13 KJV

God must have known that people would try to make salvation something they could do on their own. This is why "good" people often have a hard time accepting Christ. Because they strive to be good neighbors, don't cheat on their taxes, and love animals, they conclude that there isn't much God needs to save them from. After all, they're doing just fine on their own. They might even think that God should be happy that someone so good exists in a such a rotten world.

Good choices, however, should be an indication of

something bigger happening in your life. God gave His commands to inspire a relationship and instill a willingness to obey, and He wants you to trust Him, not yourself, for the strength to follow what He says.

A man of courage admits that he can't do good apart from God. He is willing to ask for and accept God's help to achieve something more than behavior modification. This man gets wiser with every choice as his personal relationship with his Maker transforms him from a lone wolf to a child of God.

Have you ever believed that good Christians never make mistakes? How does a relationship with God change the reason for obedience?

Be the Man
WHO IS MORE THAN A CONQUEROR

In all these things we are more than conquerors through him who loved us.

ROMANS 8:37 NIV

Romans 8:37 feels like a bold, encouraging start to a pep rally or an inspirational social media post. However, it's simply a summary of the more complex passage that precedes it.

When Paul wrote the words, "All these things," what was he talking about? To answer that question, go back a few verses and read about the adversity Christians faced. They were being charged with religious crimes, but God was defending them (verse 33). People were trying to condemn them, but God embraced them (verse 34). Paul challenged his readers the people to think, "Who shall separate us from the love of Christ?" The answer is *nothing*—not even "trouble or hardship or persecution or famine or nakedness or danger or sword" (verse 35 NIV).

Need proof? "I am convinced that neither death nor

life, neither angels nor demons, neither the present nor the future, nor any powers, neither height nor depth, nor anything else in all creation, will be able to separate us from the love of God that is in Christ Jesus our Lord" (verses 38–39 NIV).

What a powerful encouragement! You are more than a conqueror because of Jesus, His love, and the friendship He wants with you. Don't run away, hide, or seek another choice—God has already proven He will do anything to reach you. His love is yours, and no one can take it away from you.

Do you feel like a conqueror in matters of faith? Does the pursuit of God bring courage when your spirit is weak?

Be the Man
WHO COURAGEOUSLY CONFESSES

If we say that we have no sin, we deceive ourselves, and the truth is not in us. If we confess our sins, he is faithful and just to forgive us our sins, and to cleanse us from all unrighteousness.

1 JOHN 1:8-9 KJV

King Morty reigned over a faraway enchanted land. When one of his subjects even thought about breaking his rules, King Morty somehow knew. He would then bring those subjects before his throne and demand an explanation. There were more prisoners than merchants in his kingdom because Morty prosecuted violators swiftly and to the full extent of his law.

Did these lawbreakers love King Morty, or were they afraid of him? He knew their most private thoughts but knew nothing of forgiveness, grace, and mercy.

God also knows your every thought. He knows when you break His law—but unlike Morty, He waits for you to come to Him. He wants you to tell Him what you've done or even thought. You can't hide anything from God, yet He's willing to forgive, wiping your criminal history clean with His faithful love.

God isn't winking at your sin as if it's unimportant; He's holding out a helping hand and is willing to walk with you toward obedience.

Under the tyranny of King Morty, who punishes every infraction swiftly and mercilessly, being a man of courage would be impossible. God, however, counts you as a friend, so you can come to Him and tell Him each time you blow it. Give him the details, experience His forgiveness, then remember Jesus' words: "Go, and sin no more" (John 8:11 KJV).

How is God's response to confession different than humanity's? Why is forgiveness essential to trusting God?

Be the Man
WHO IS REDEEMED
BY RELATIONSHIP

He asked them, "But who do you say I am?" Simon Peter answered, "You are the Messiah, the Son of the living God." Jesus replied, "You are blessed, Simon son of John, because my Father in heaven has revealed this to you. You did not learn this from any human being. I say to you that you are Peter (which means 'rock'), and upon this rock I will build my church, and all the powers of hell will not conquer it."

MATTHEW 16:15–18 NLT

If anyone had a chronic case of foot-in-mouth disease, it was Peter. He was a master at promise breaking, and he would often commit himself to actions he wasn't prepared to take. This disciple was impulsive, yet Peter likely mistook this flaw for boldness.

Jesus saw all of this, making what He told Peter in today's verse even more amazing: The Lord wanted His disciple to know that the church would grow with Peter! This disciple would need to know that even when the church was battered and bruised, it would not be conquered. . .and this promise-breaking disciple would be instrumental in its success.

As Peter preached the good news, there had to be nights when he remembered his betrayals and foolish promises. He now realized that personal bravado could never replace God's strength.

Peter's story can encourage you, and not just because you can say, "I did better than him." No, his story proves that new life is a growing, daily process. You continuously learn to identify errors, speak life, and forgive, leaving your sinful choices further behind and redeeming your relationships with imperfect people.

God works through forgiven, hopeful, and courageous men like you.

How does it feel to know that your greatest mistakes do nothing to stop God from working in your life? What encouragement do you find in the life of Peter?

Be the Man
WHO ONLY SPEAKS
WHEN NECESSARY

Is anyone among you in trouble? Let them pray. Is anyone happy? Let them sing songs of praise.

JAMES 5:13 NIV

Sometimes, courage means realizing that some of your thoughts are better left unsaid. Other times, it means speaking the truth when every other mouth is shut. But it *always* takes wisdom to know which kind of courage you need to use in each situation.

Courageous silence often means checking God's Word before you speak. Then, if you've decided something needs to be said, courageous conversation will bring God into the subject even when others don't want to hear about Him.

Ecclesiastes 5:2 (NIV) helps clarify the idea of courageous silence: "Do not be quick with your mouth, do not be hasty in your heart to utter anything before God. God is in heaven and you are on earth, so let your words be few."

Proverbs 31:8–9 (NIV), however, tells when your words

might prove helpful: "Speak up for those who cannot speak for themselves, for the rights of all who are destitute. Speak up and judge fairly; defend the rights of the poor and needy."

It's easy to share opinions about things you don't understand. And sometimes, you might even be able to speak the truth, but your timing may be horrible.

When you get into God's Word, you'll grow better at discerning when something is important enough to speak about. . .and when you should allow your jaw to rest.

Is it easier for you to speak up or keep silent? Why? How can you learn to tell when you should use your words to honor God and help others?

Be the Man
WHO REFUSES TO LET SIN DOMINATE

Let not sin therefore reign in your mortal body, that ye should obey it in the lusts thereof. Neither yield ye your members as instruments of unrighteousness unto sin: but yield yourselves unto God, as those that are alive from the dead, and your members as instruments of righteousness unto God. For sin shall not have dominion over you: for ye are not under the law, but under grace.

ROMANS 6:12–14 KJV

Sin is bossy, but it's not your boss. It has power, but only the power you give it.

Your adversary will try his best to convince you that the choice to sin is natural and fun. If he can convince you that God has been holding out on you, the allure of sin in your life will be enhanced even more.

God's grace is more powerful than the laws you break, so your sins don't need to interfere with your relationship with Him. But does this mean you have a free pass to sin? The apostle Paul gave a simple, eloquent answer in

Romans 6:2 (KJV): "God forbid. How shall we, that are dead to sin, live any longer therein?"

Sin can seem like a default response when you're at your weakest, but God gives the strength you need to resist. You don't need to live by the old adage that forgiveness is preferable to permission.

A courageous man refuses to dance on the edge of unrighteousness. He's not concerned about what he can get away with; rather, he wants only to do the right thing. He doesn't want to constantly wonder if he needs forgiveness—he's committed to learning what God wants. He stops chasing sin and continues his passionate pursuit of God.

Does sin sometimes seem like the resident bully in your decision making? Why is it liberating to know that just because sin makes a suggestion, you don't have to take it?

Be the Man
WHO SETS COURAGEOUS BOUNDARIES

Shadrach, Meshach, and Abednego replied, "O Nebuchadnezzar, we do not need to defend ourselves before you. If we are thrown into the blazing furnace, the God whom we serve is able to save us. He will rescue us from your power, Your Majesty. But even if he doesn't, we want to make it clear to you, Your Majesty, that we will never serve your gods or worship the gold statue you have set up."

DANIEL 3:16–18 NLT

The value of well-chosen words should not be taken lightly.

When King Nebuchadnezzar required everyone to worship a statue, he may not have considered the implications of such a law (the idea that he could determine who was a god) nor the penalty for disobedience (death).

Three friends, however, refused to compromise. They knew their choice could result in death, but they didn't believe the king was equal with God. So these men brought truth to the king, choosing their words carefully.

They openly rejected the king's command, stating

that they were committed to serving God instead. They knew the king couldn't decide their fate—only God could do that.

The angry Nebuchadnezzar pronounced a death sentence, but God enacted a rescue plan. The king brought heat, but God brought perspective. In the end, the brash king boldly declared, "Praise to the God of Shadrach, Meshach, and Abednego! He sent his angel to rescue his servants who trusted in him. They defied the king's command and were willing to die rather than serve or worship any god except their own God" (Daniel 3:28 NLT).

Courageous boundaries give the world an impressive example.

In the face of mounting pressure to comply with sin, are you courageous enough to resist? What can you do to establish visible, courageous boundaries?

Be the Man
WHO FOLLOWS THE
KING OF COURAGE

"Do not let your hearts be troubled. You believe in God; believe also in me. My Father's house has many rooms; if that were not so, would I have told you that I am going there to prepare a place for you? And if I go and prepare a place for you, I will come back and take you to be with me that you also may be where I am. You know the way to the place where I am going. . . . I am the way and the truth and the life. No one comes to the Father except through me."

JOHN 14:1-4, 6 NIV

Can you name a person with more courage than Jesus? He left His glorious life in heaven, knowing He would be betrayed, disbelieved, mocked, and killed. Each day, He had the burden of knowing all that would happen. His life was a countdown toward intense pain and suffering.

Even more, Jesus knew that many would reject His message. Many didn't want to hear it, and they certainly didn't want to believe. The Jews vehemently opposed the idea that God would come for anyone who was not a Jew.

The rest of the world struggled because of the many gods they worshipped. They would need an incredible amount of faith to believe in one God and follow Him alone.

Jesus showed courage in sharing such inconceivable truth. Consequently, people are following His example by sharing that same news today.

Remember: Jesus won't ask you to do something He hasn't done. The King of courage boldly proclaimed the good news, so feel free to repeat His message.

Have you ever tried to make excuses for not following Jesus' courageous example? If so, how can you learn to defeat these insecurities with the truth?

Be the Man
WHO CHOOSES A
PAIN-FREE FUTURE

And I heard a great voice out of heaven saying, Behold, the tabernacle of God is with men, and he will dwell with them, and they shall be his people, and God himself shall be with them, and be their God. God shall wipe away all tears from their eyes; and there shall be no more death, neither sorrow, nor crying, neither shall there be any more pain: for the former things are passed away.

REVELATION 21:3–4 KJV

You've probably heard the expression, "If it seems too good to be true it probably is." A calorie-free cake, an unbreakable toy, a camera that takes perfect selfies—all of these miracle inventions get peddled by late night infomercials and shady websites each day, so we've learned to keep our suspicion antenna raised high.

In a world of high expectations and false promises, it's not really surprising that some of God's promises seem unbelievable. It takes courage to believe in a future in which no therapists, hospitals, or funeral homes are needed. But that's just a sneak peek at heaven.

The courage you bring to this celestial view is faith—and this faith will not disappoint. Jesus said, "In my Father's house are many mansions: if it were not so, I would have told you. I go to prepare a place for you. And if I go and prepare a place for you, I will come again, and receive you unto myself; that where I am, there ye may be also" (John 14:2–3 KJV).

If this sounds too good to be true, just remember: God has never broken a promise.

Do you find it hard to believe in a heaven you've never seen? How does the hope of heaven renew your courage?

Be the Man
WHO LEAVES THE
FUNHOUSE BEHIND

They stumble because they do not obey God's word, and so they meet the fate that was planned for them. But you are not like that, for you are a chosen people. You are royal priests, a holy nation, God's very own possession. As a result, you can show others the goodness of God, for he called you out of the darkness into his wonderful light.

1 PETER 2:8–9 NLT

Have you ever been in a carnival funhouse? It was filled with darkness, trap doors, and mirrors that distorted your perception of who you really are. It was designed to be amusing, but soon, you started feeling lost and discombobulated (a fancy word that just means "confused"; look it up!). Slowly, your confusion turned to awkwardness and discomfort. You tried to leave, but you couldn't find the exit.

Finally stumbling out of the funhouse reintroduced you to reality. Darkness became light and distortion gave way to solid shape and substance.

You have been chosen by God, and you get to choose Him. He called you from life's funhouse, so you never need to experience discombobulation again.

Grab hold of the courage you need to leave your old life's distortion behind in the adversary's funhouse. Discard the lies you accepted as truth. It will be hard, but the results will be liberating. You will come to love this new life. Any allure to the old funhouse will become more and more absurd.

People are leaving the devil's funhouse every day. If you haven't joined them yet, today is the perfect time to start.

Has the spiritual funhouse ever left you discombobulated? Do you choose each day to reject the funhouse in favor of God's wonderful light?

Be the Man
WHO BELIEVES IN HOPE

Isaiah says, "The Root of Jesse will spring up, one who will arise to rule over the nations; in him the Gentiles will hope." May the God of hope fill you with all joy and peace as you trust in him, so that you may overflow with hope by the power of the Holy Spirit.

ROMANS 15:12–13 NIV

In the movie *Pinocchio*, a small cricket urges the title character to find a star and make a wish. If only reality were that simple!

Sadly, there's no evidence that stars, which are just balls of hydrogen and helium, have ever been able to grant wishes. . .but they do recognize God as Creator. The Lord Himself said "the morning stars sang together" when He laid the earth's foundation (Job 38:7 NIV).

The God who made the stars wants you to put your hope in Him. The stars are His creation. He is the Creator. That's a huge difference. You shouldn't honor a piece of art and not the artist, celebrate a song over the songwriter, or praise a meal without acknowledging the cook.

The hope God gives isn't a wish-on-a-star kind of hope, and it's not something you can manufacture on your own. Rather, it's the assurance that all His promises will come to pass. When you accept His hope, you have access to joy and peace.

There's no downside to courageously consuming a full dose of God's hope.

Do you regularly access God's real hope?
How is this hope different from a wish?

Be the Man
WHO HAS A SECOND WIND

No discipline is enjoyable while it is happening—it's painful! But afterward there will be a peaceful harvest of right living for those who are trained in this way. Take a new grip with your tired hands and strengthen your weak knees. Mark out a straight path for your feet so that those who are weak and lame will not fall but become strong.

HEBREWS 12:11–13 NLT

The term *second wind* originated in the 1830s and is used to describe an unexpected burst of strength in times of weariness.

A second wind inspires you to continue moving forward. It somehow turns exhaustion into energy, reigniting your passion. You've probably felt it while doing anything from cross country running to lawn care, and you might even encounter it on a recurring basis.

Galatians 6:9 (NLT) perfectly describes the idea behind a second wind: "So let's not get tired of doing what is good. At just the right time we will reap a harvest of blessing if we don't give up." Here, God provides the purpose (doing good) and the outcome (blessings).

You can walk even when the steps are hard and run when it seems your spiritual lungs are on fire—all you have to do is access the second wind that the Spirit offers. Then you can continue pursuing righteousness without the need to turn aside or take a break.

A man of courage moves past the desire to call it a day before his work is done. He presses on, even when he's certain he can't. He believes that a spiritual second wind will come soon.

Have you ever felt a second wind in your spiritual life? Why is it comforting to know God makes all things possible?

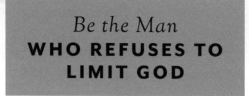

Be the Man
WHO REFUSES TO LIMIT GOD

Then they cried out with a loud voice, and stopped their ears, and ran upon him with one accord, and cast [Stephen] out of the city, and stoned him: and the witnesses laid down their clothes at a young man's feet, whose name was Saul.

ACTS 7:57–58 KJV

While reading a novel, you may have noticed that the author provided time-released information, slowly filling in the blanks but leaving you hungry for more. Often, such books will drop names and crucial bits of context like breadcrumbs before revealing the twist at the end.

Guess what? The Bible uses this strategy too. Acts 7:58, for instance, is about Stephen, a devout follower of Jesus who was "full of faith and power, [and] did great wonders and miracles among the people" (Acts 6:8 KJV). In this chapter, this strong and faithful follower was killed for his faith.

Maybe you noticed the name drop at the end of verse 58 (KJV): "Witnesses laid down their clothes at a young man's feet, whose name was Saul." Who was Saul? Why did he hate Christians? Is he important to the story?

Well, the author later reveals that Saul was a Pharisee who thought Christians were misguided at best and dangerous at worst. He was all for eradicating them, so he was probably thrilled to be in charge of the religious protesters' coats.

But soon, Saul would meet Jesus. Nothing—not even his name—would remain the same. Jesus renamed him Paul, and he became an apostle.

In a single verse, we read of a courageous man who died for his faith as well as a man who would soon receive that faith. As Paul's story proves, we should never view anyone—even the worst of sinners—as beyond redemption.

No one is too bad for God to rescue.

Do you ever doubt that God is willing to save anyone? How can this story of Stephen and Saul help erase these doubts?

Be the Man
WHO TRUSTS THE
ONE HE FOLLOWS

*The LORD is my light and my salvation—whom shall I fear?
The LORD is the stronghold of my life—of whom shall I be
afraid? When the wicked advance against me to devour me, it
is my enemies and my foes who will stumble and fall. Though
an army besiege me, my heart will not fear; though war break
out against me, even then I will be confident.*

PSALM 27:1–3 NIV

Pick a cause—any cause. It could be one that you or a
friend identifies with or cares deeply about. Now that
you have that cause in mind, how do its supporters show
that it's important to them? Some might send a check,
others might volunteer to help bring awareness to the
cause, and still others might boycott anything that's
opposed to the cause, writing letters to the newspaper
or posting online about their disapproval. Rarely,
however, will someone die for a cause.

King David had a cause, and that cause was God.
Because the king stood for God, God helped him.

Eventually, the king concluded that his confidence could find secure lodging in God's goodness. Armed with God's love and protection, he could face a whole army of foes.

And he did. Often.

When you allow your life to represent the cause of Christ, any adversity along the way just draws you closer to the one you follow.

The willingness to stand for this cause is the wisdom to be confident.

How much do you believe in the cause of Christ? What can you do today to demonstrate your full devotion to this cause?

Be the Man
WHO DOESN'T TRUST
THE WRONG THING

Teach those who are rich in this world not to be proud and not to trust in their money, which is so unreliable. Their trust should be in God, who richly gives us all we need for our enjoyment.

1 TIMOTHY 6:17 NLT

You can't be a man of courage when the thing you trust the most is unreliable. You probably wouldn't be courageous enough to take a cross country trip in a dilapidated car that just passed 350,000 miles. You wouldn't enter a weightlifting competition if the biggest thing you've lifted lately is a twin pack of snack cakes. You wouldn't suggest the help of a friend if that friend has never shown up to help you.

You either have courage or you don't. You are either confident in God's abilities or doubtful.

Before you form your opinion, look at the facts: God is supreme (Isaiah 44:6–8), eternal (Psalm 48:14), loving (John 3:16), perfect (Psalm 18:30), merciful (Ephesians 2:4–5), good (Psalm 100:5), forgiving (Daniel 9:9), and understanding (Psalm 139:1–6).

When you have God, you have every reason to be a man of courage. God is not faulty, unreliable, or shifty. He never has to say, "Sorry I wasn't there for you today. I'll try harder tomorrow."

In other words, God's not just a little nice addition to your life—He's everything you need. God can do everything that you can't. That's why you come to Him, read His words, and ask for His help.

Today, refuse to trust the wrong thing. Let God give you courage instead.

What do you lack that God offers?
Do you try finding courage in Him alone?

Be the Man
WHO RETURNS AND RESTS

For thus saith the Lord GOD, the Holy One of Israel; In returning and rest shall ye be saved; in quietness and in confidence shall be your strength: and ye would not. . . . And therefore will the LORD wait, that he may be gracious unto you, and therefore will he be exalted, that he may have mercy upon you: for the LORD is a God of judgment: blessed are all they that wait for him.

ISAIAH 30:15, 18 KJV

As life churns by at breakneck speeds, the gift of rest seems perfect. Sometimes, this rest is a physical timeout—a welcome relief from the mind-numbing, sickening effects of stress.

God offered the people of Israel this kind of rest, but first they had to leave their fast-paced tilt-a-whirl of sinful choices and return to Him. Their timeout came in the form of captivity, the horrors of which slowly moved their hearts back to God. When they finally returned home, they were changed.

Humanity is guilty of rejecting God's offer of heart

recalibration. Thinking you know more than God is a common condition. When God says, "Come back to me," we look at our schedules and don't seem to find an opening until the twelfth of Never.

Ask yourself: Is it wise to reject an offer from the only one who knows how to fix you?

Do you routinely seek the rest God has for you? Whenever you stray, how does coming back to God shorten any unwanted spiritual timeouts?

Be the Man
WHO MAKES GOD WELCOME

Remember those earlier days after you had received the light, when you endured in a great conflict full of suffering. Sometimes you were publicly exposed to insult and persecution; at other times you stood side by side with those who were so treated. You suffered along with those in prison and joyfully accepted the confiscation of your property, because you knew that you yourselves had better and lasting possessions. Do not throw away your confidence; it will be richly rewarded.

HEBREWS 10:32–35 NIV

A private faith is a faith that lacks confidence. Many men will agree that faith belongs with family and freedom, but how often do they talk about faith compared to the other two? Often, people just have to assume a Christian man has faith because no one hears much about it.

Some claim that St. Francis of Assisi said, "Preach the gospel at all times. Use words if necessary." The problem with this quote is that it suggests that your life example is all that you really need in order to share Jesus. If that were true, what use would there be for the Great Commission (Matthew 28:16–20)?

Courage is a megaphone for your faith. It learns when to infuse conversations with spiritual truth and is never embarrassed to mention God.

If you are passionate about a sports team, you will spit out the scores and stats, forming instant friendships among strangers. But what about when it comes to God? Are you confident and courageous enough to bring Him up in conversations with others? You don't need to preach to bring God into a topic.

If you throw away the confidence God gave you, something else will invariably replace it. Don't invite fear into your conversation—be courageous with your words.

Why is it so hard sometimes to talk to people about God? How can you be more confident in today's conversations?

Be the Man
WHO KEEPS THE DIVIDING WALL BROKEN

Deceit fills hearts that are plotting evil; joy fills hearts that are planning peace! No harm comes to the godly, but the wicked have their fill of trouble. The LORD detests lying lips, but he delights in those who tell the truth.

PROVERBS 12:20-22 NLT

Why do you think God detests lying lips? Is "thou shalt not bear false witness" (or, in other words, *lie*) just an arbitrary command?

Probably not. Maybe the reason God hates lying is because of the effect it has on courage. Without courage, it's easy to believe that God is so harsh and cruel that you have to hide behind lies for safety. But do you honestly think God doesn't know. . .or couldn't find out?

The truth is, God forgives any sin you confess and then removes it from your record. He strongly desires to see you get back on the right path—*His* path. Manipulating the truth only leads to confusion and frustration. Lies require energy that could be diverted to God's plan for you.

Detesting lies seems more like a logical response now, doesn't it?

Truth tellers get God's approval. They advance His message, refuse to waste time, and recognize the absurdity of running from God. These people are courageous and confident, refusing to let lies erect a dividing wall between their heart and God's Spirit.

Each of God's rules has a purpose, and it often involves improving your relationship with Him—as well as with others.

Has lying ever affected your friendship with God? Have you ever considered that God detests lies because He knows they hurt you?

Be the Man
WHO WANTS TO
KNOW MORE

As a dog returns to its vomit, so a fool repeats his foolishness. There is more hope for fools than for people who think they are wise.

PROVERBS 26:11-12 NLT

Imagine this scenario: Alexander Graham Bell, Thomas Edison, Albert Einstein, and a host of the world's greatest minds are attending a party, demonstrating their inventions and formulas. Suddenly, a guy walks in and starts using big words and flowery speech. But it soon becomes evident to everyone that this man actually has no idea what he's talking about. He's just trying to fit in. The brilliant attendees could contradict the visitor quickly and easily—but they'd rather stand by and watch as the man digs himself deeper and deeper into humiliation.

When you think you know it all, you belittle everyone else. You feel certain no one can teach you anything. You might even tell God that His work in your life is no longer mysterious because you already understand it. God, however, takes greater delight in those who admit their thinking is foolish than those who believe they could teach Him a thing or two. No one can match wits with God.

It always takes courage to admit you could use some wisdom—to admit that you've played the critically acclaimed role of a fool. But such a confession will prove to everyone that you can listen without trying to impress.

Be a courageous fool who realizes that learning is the best part of knowing.

When you approach God, do you behave like a teachable fool or a know-it-all? How wise do you think you are compared to God's knowledge?

Be the Man
WHO CHOOSES TO GATHER

[Nehemiah prayed,] "We have acted very wickedly toward you. We have not obeyed the commands, decrees and laws you gave your servant Moses. Remember the instruction you gave your servant Moses, saying, 'If you are unfaithful, I will scatter you among the nations, but if you return to me and obey my commands, then even if your exiled people are at the farthest horizon, I will gather them from there and bring them to the place I have chosen as a dwelling for my Name.'"

NEHEMIAH 1:7–9 NIV

During the divinely foretold scattering, the disobedience of sinners was punished by a trustworthy God.

Nehemiah prayed that this scattering would one day turn into a gathering, in which Nehemiah's family, neighbors and friends would return home. Home, however, wasn't what it once was. The temple sat empty, the walls of the city lay in piles of rubble, and few people lived there anymore. For God to bring Nehemiah's family home, they would need something to come home to.

Nehemiah's courage started with a bold prayer, and then it led to a conversation with the king who held the people of Israel captive. Surprisingly, the king granted him the privilege of rebuilding the city walls!

One man of courage thought mourning the state of affairs was not enough—something had to be done, and he was willing to step up to the plate. Consequently, God took this man's courage and displaced a nation's collective despair.

Today, the rubble of your broken life can be reclaimed by God, and the scattered parts can be gathered. All you must do is courageously cooperate with God's reclamation project for your life.

How do you react when the odds are against you?
How will you trust God to lead you away from
fear and toward the fulfillment of His plan?

Be the Man
WHO ACCEPTS STRENGTH

Then there came again and touched me one like the appearance of a man, and he strengthened me, and said, O man greatly beloved, fear not: peace be unto thee, be strong, yea, be strong. And when he had spoken unto me, I was strengthened, and said, Let my lord speak; for thou hast strengthened me.

DANIEL 10:18–19 KJV

Telling yourself that you are strong is just wishful thinking. Lying to yourself will never make these whispers true.

Men have been lying to themselves since the beginning of time, telling themselves that they actually are whatever they want to be. And almost all of these things they tell themselves have one thing in common—courage. No man wants to be weak.

If God says you are strong, then you are strong—stronger than you could ever be on your own. You can't equate your workout at the gym with true strength. God doesn't care how much weight you can lift. Even if you could bench press a tractor, you'd never be as impressive as the Creator of the universe, the one who flung stars into space, carved out canyons, and still listens to your voice.

God gave Daniel strength, and Daniel knew it because he could pay attention to God without fear. When you think about how impressive God is—how vast His power, creation, and love for us extends—it's easy to become overwhelmed. However, don't let this weakness replace the courage you need to approach Him. God gives us this courage because He always chooses friendship over intimidation.

How can you gain strength by thinking about how amazing God truly is? How does your friendship with God give you strength?

Be the Man
WHO WELCOMES
THE IMPOSSIBLE

Sing to the LORD with grateful praise; make music to our God on the harp. He covers the sky with clouds; he supplies the earth with rain and makes grass grow on the hills. . . . His pleasure is not in the strength of the horse, nor his delight in the legs of the warrior; the LORD delights in those who fear him, who put their hope in his unfailing love.

PSALM 147:7–8, 10–11 NIV

You are a warrior because God made you one. You can do nothing on your own. Without His help, even your best efforts look embarrassing and misguided.

If you're like most men, you probably like to show off your warrior identity. But looks can be deceiving. How often have you trembled beneath a confident pose? Felt your mouth turn dry as cotton while you spoke?

When you say you can handle anything but know deep down that you're bragging about the impossible, just remember that you serve the God of the impossible. In Jeremiah 32:27 (NIV), He asked, "I am the LORD, the

God of all mankind. Is anything too hard for me?" The answer will always be no.

No amount of physical strength can compare to God's power. Working out doesn't hurt, but it's not what God delights in when He looks at you. Respect God and put every bit of trust you have in His love, which never quits, breaks, or stops reaching for you.

Life can seem like asking a five-year-old to complete a thousand-piece puzzle by lunchtime—impossible. Yet when God gives you an assignment, you must leave your insecurities behind, trusting that He'll provide the help you need.

How scared are you of failure? Does the word impossible inspire you to trust God even more?

Be the Man
WHO IS THIRSTY FOR MORE

O God, thou art my God; early will I seek thee: my soul thirsteth for thee, my flesh longeth for thee in a dry and thirsty land, where no water is; to see thy power and thy glory, so as I have seen thee in the sanctuary. Because thy lovingkindness is better than life, my lips shall praise thee. Thus will I bless thee while I live: I will lift up my hands in thy name.

PSALM 63:1-4 KJV

In the movie *Castaway*, Tom Hanks plays a survivor on a deserted island. He's surrounded by water but has little to drink. His lips are chapped, his voice is hoarse, and the appearance of his entire body screams that he needs to be refreshed.

Similarly, King David described what it was like to be on a proverbial desert island, far away from God. Everything about the experience filled the king with bold desperation to return to his source of nourishment. His spiritual tank was empty, and he knew God was the ingredient missing.

Do you want God that much? Or do you sometimes

think of Him as a crutch—an item to pick up only after all other options have failed? Here's the catch: there never were any other options—you need His help for *everything*.

It's okay to recognize that you're thirsty for spiritual water that only God can offer. This, in fact, is the only good response. Being needy is great when it leads to the God who meets needs.

You seek God because God satisfies. Longing for His relief isn't a sign of weakness—it's the perfect approach for a man of courage who refuses to stay in the desert.

Do you find it hard to admit you can't do everything on your own? Are you courageous enough to show your desperation to God?

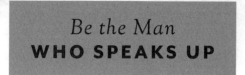

Be the Man
WHO SPEAKS UP

The sayings of King Lemuel contain this message, which his mother taught him. O my son, O son of my womb, O son of my vows. . . . Speak up for those who cannot speak for themselves; ensure justice for those being crushed. Yes, speak up for the poor and helpless, and see that they get justice.

PROVERBS 31:1-2, 8-9 NLT

As Mr. Smith stood to speak about greed and corruption, some thought he was foolishly throwing away his political career. Others worked overtime to push him over the edge. A few, however, stood in his corner, knowing his efforts might prove futile yet strongly hoping his words would be heard. Perhaps Mr. Smith could do what no one had yet been able to do.

If this story sounds familiar, that's because it's the plot of the classic movie *Mr. Smith Goes to Washington*, starring Jimmy Stewart as the title character.

You too have a certain amount of influence, large or small, wherever you go. It takes guts to speak up for others, especially when you feel no one else is listening.

It's always easier, after all, to just stay silent. However, for those misunderstood, mistreated, poverty-stricken souls, your voice may be the only hope in sight.

These opportunities aren't just limited to social programs—everyone, including you, has an opportunity to change a life. When you speak for those who lack a voice, new friendships start to form, leading to new opportunities to share God's life-changing message of salvation. That opportunity can change eternity for someone in need.

Maybe that's why you're here—people need to know that God has sent help.

Do you feel uncomfortable speaking up for those who have no voice? If so, how can you change your outlook by identifying with those in need?

Be the Man
WHO FINDS PURPOSE IN STRUGGLE

But he said to me, "My grace is sufficient for you, for my power is made perfect in weakness." Therefore I will boast all the more gladly about my weaknesses, so that Christ's power may rest on me. That is why, for Christ's sake, I delight in weaknesses, in insults, in hardships, in persecutions, in difficulties. For when I am weak, then I am strong.

2 CORINTHIANS 12:9-10 NIV

Say your name out loud, and then follow it with the words "is weak." Feels good, doesn't it? No? Well, that's understandable—nobody wants to feel that way.

The apostle Paul, however, was secure enough in his spiritual walk to admit that he was weak, that insults didn't faze him, that hardships were to be expected, and that persecutions no longer caused him to run.

How is that possible? You might think. *Did Paul have a martyr complex?*

No. He just had a good grasp on what's important.

Paul didn't prefer these abysmal conditions. As a child,

he didn't dream of one day wading through an endless slog of trials. But he endured these conditions for one reason—the gospel of Christ.

Without a purpose, Paul would've had zero courage for these trials. He would've found it easy to run away. But in running away, he would've missed some profound encounters with God—and an opportunity to impact billions in the future with his life's story.

All of your suffering has a purpose, even when you don't know what the purpose may be. Christ is the master planner, and He doesn't always share His secrets. You may discover some of them in time, or you may not.

All you need is courage. . .and the simple faith to believe that God is using your trouble for good.

Do you find yourself running whenever trouble comes your way? If so, how can you gain a sense of purpose to provide the courage you need?

Be the Man
WHO STANDS FOR TRUTH

The Jews took up stones again to stone him. Jesus answered them, Many good works have I shewed you from my Father; for which of those works do ye stone me? The Jews answered him, saying, For a good work we stone thee not; but for blasphemy; and because that thou, being a man, makest thyself God.

JOHN 10:31–33 KJV

Sometimes, the desire for privacy is understandable. A spy, after all, won't wear a t-shirt advertising his identity, and a member of the royal family won't wear a tiara to the shopping mall. Other times, however, a refusal to speak the truth is tantamount to lying.

When Jesus came to earth, He felt and experienced human emotions. Each day, he probably wrestled with the temptation to keep His divine identity silent. Yet Jesus was the supreme man of courage—truth was consistent with Him, whether it made His audience uncomfortable or not. His words directly challenged the falsehoods of His day.

Many people struggled to accept the truth that Jesus

spoke—even His own family. Others, such as the Pharisees, outright rejected it, hating it so much that they eventually killed Him. His kind of truth sounded so unbelievable that His enemies saw no other option than to forcibly silence it. Only a few saw the truth behind His message.

Today, strive to know, live, and share the truth. Jesus brought it, proved it, and left it for you to explore. Be a man of courage, and don't keep truth to yourself.

What can you do today to courageously share the truth? With whom will you share it first?

Be the Man
WHO MOVES FROM QUESTIONS TO PRAISE

The Sovereign LORD is my strength! He makes me as surefooted as a deer, able to tread upon the heights.

HABAKKUK 3:19 NLT

Many scholars believe that Habakkuk worked in the temple and composed worshipful songs, some of which are written down in his book.

But before the praise began, this songwriter was filled with questions and complaints: "How long, O LORD, must I call for help? But you do not listen! 'Violence is everywhere!' I cry, but you do not come to save" (Habakkuk 1:2 NLT).

God, however, answered the songsmith: "I am doing something in your own day, something you wouldn't believe even if someone told you about it" (Habakkuk 1:5 NLT).

These words rocked the prophet's world. God's plan, he discovered, *included* the Israelites' captivity. The end result would be much better than letting people continually break His laws.

As a result, this is what the prophet concluded:

Even though the fig trees have no blossoms, and there are no grapes on the vines; even though the olive crop fails, and the fields lie empty and barren; even though the flocks die in the fields, and the cattle barns are empty, yet I will rejoice in the LORD! I will be joyful in the God of my salvation! The Sovereign LORD is my strength!

HABAKKUK 3:17–19 NLT

Even in the face of total failure, Habakkuk knew that God could be trusted to bring joy and strength—and that the fruits of His plan were just around the corner.

Today, take comfort in this strengthening glimpse of God's goodness.

Has God ever used your questions and complaints to alter your opinion? How can you turn bad news into an occasion for worship?

Be the Man
WHO GIVES IT ALL HE'S GOT

He asked him, "Of all the commandments, which is the most important?" "The most important one," answered Jesus, "is this: 'Hear, O Israel: The Lord our God, the Lord is one. Love the Lord your God with all your heart and with all your soul and with all your mind and with all your strength.'"

MARK 12:28-30 NIV

Who doesn't love a good circus act? There's just something so satisfying about seeing dangerous stunts and unusual sideshows—it's hard to find these experiences anywhere else.

Frank "Cannonball" Richards wasn't your typical penny carnival performer, however. He had a cannonball fired into his stomach. . .twice a day! He started by allowing spectators to punch him in the gut, worked his way up to having sledgehammers hurled at his stomach, and eventually upgraded to cannonballs.

Frank didn't start as strong as he finished. He just found something he was passionate about and applied everything he had to pursuing it.

Your Christian life takes a similar path. While no one is asking you to take a cannonball to the gut, God *is* asking you to pursue Him with your heart's emotions, your soul's conviction, your mind's intellect, and every ounce of your body's strength. Combining these four things in your life is guaranteed to make you a man of courage.

A courageous Christian doesn't leave himself out of the running or set himself aside when God says, "Get going."

God is the one who gave what you've got, and He wants you to make the most of it for Him today. So bring all the willingness you can, and allow God to make up for your personal deficits with His goodness.

Be a full-time follower.

Do you sometimes feel as if you don't have enough for God? How can you increase your passion as you pursue Him?

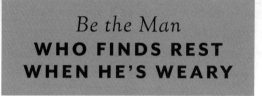

Come unto me, all ye that labour and are heavy laden, and I will give you rest. Take my yoke upon you, and learn of me; for I am meek and lowly in heart: and ye shall find rest unto your souls. For my yoke is easy, and my burden is light.

MATTHEW 11:28–30 KJV

A team of eight strong men gathered in Ukraine. Using nothing but ropes and their muscles, they pulled the world's heaviest cargo plane—which weighed a whopping 628,300 pounds—fourteen feet in just over a minute. Talk about a group of modern day Atlases!

Physical exertion can be tortuous, but believe it or not, emotional or spiritual exhaustion is even worse. Whether your battles are public or private, the outcome will be disastrous unless you let God step in. Contrary to popular belief, the Bible never says, "God helps those who help themselves," and neither does it teach, "God never gives you more than you can handle." God *absolutely* gives His people more than they can handle! Often, God allows you to become overwhelmed so that you'll run to Him for rest.

God wants you to learn endurance and perseverance, not to be broken by exhaustion. Believing otherwise is a surefire path to weariness and fear.

Tug on the rope as long as you like, but by yourself, you'll never move far enough to reach your goal—only God has the strength you need.

How does exhaustion negatively affect you? When you're overwhelmed, what's your first instinct—to work harder or to give it to God?

Be the Man
WHO ACCEPTS GOD'S PROTECTION

Pray, too, that we will be rescued from wicked and evil people, for not everyone is a believer. The Lord is faithful; he will strengthen you and guard you from the evil one.

2 THESSALONIANS 3:2–3 NLT

Satan was nearly salivating at the opportunity to bring a faithful man, Job, to ruin. When God commended Job's faithfulness, Satan boldly jumped at the chance to prove how irresistible his corrupting power truly was. He came before God with one request: "You have always put a wall of protection around him and his home and his property. You have made him prosper in everything he does. Look how rich he is! But reach out and take away everything he has, and he will surely curse you to your face!" (Job 1:10–11 NLT).

If you're thinking that God would decline this request, think again! God actually allowed Satan to give Job more than he could handle. Satan sought out everything that he believed caused Job to trust God—and he destroyed it. But while Job struggled to understand, He still chose to trust God. And God guarded Job's life from the devil's influence.

God didn't abandon Job, and He will never abandon you. The trouble you face is not unusual—wherever sin exists, pain is never far behind. Think of it this way: even if only one person in the entire world was capable of sinning (which is impossible; see Romans 3:23), the sin of that single individual would still bring trouble to everyone else.

That's why we must trust God to gain courage: He, not any of us, is leading the way. All we need to do is follow Him and accept the protection He offers.

How often does "trying harder" actually work?
Have you surrendered your struggles to God,
knowing He can protect you from the "evil one"?

Be the Man
WHO RECOGNIZES HIS DAD

The LORD is my strength and my shield; my heart trusts in him, and he helps me. My heart leaps for joy, and with my song I praise him. The LORD is the strength of his people, a fortress of salvation for his anointed one. Save your people and bless your inheritance; be their shepherd and carry them forever.

PSALM 28:7-9 NIV

You've likely encountered a boy who shows a great deal of respect for his "Daddy." Some boys believe their dads are invincible—there is no one wiser, stronger, or more trustworthy than this man. This boy might even believe his dad is like a comic book hero. He's larger than life, and the boy wants everyone to know.

You can have this kind of response to God, who helps you do so much more than you can on your own. He brings protection with Him, and He knows how to use it. As a result, maybe you'll want to shout, "Hey, look everybody, this is my God!"

If you don't see God this way, can you honestly say you're courageous? And even if you think you're pretty tough on your own, are you bold about things that really matter? It's easy to depend on something other than God—including yourself—until the illusion of safety suddenly falls through.

If you know God and see Him for who He is, then you can stand in the face of your most difficult days with the strength only He can provide.

Smile while you remind yourself, "God is my Dad!"

Does it feel strange for you to speak openly about God as a good Father? How can you brag about God's goodness today?

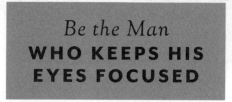

Why take ye thought for raiment? Consider the lilies of the field, how they grow; they toil not, neither do they spin: And yet I say unto you, That even Solomon in all his glory was not arrayed like one of these. Wherefore, if God so clothe the grass of the field, which to day is, and to morrow is cast into the oven, shall he not much more clothe you, O ye of little faith? Take no thought, saying, What shall we eat? or, What shall we drink? or, Wherewithal shall we be clothed?

MATTHEW 6:28–31 KJV

Have you ever wondered where your rent money is going to come from? If you have enough spare change for the dollar menu? If so, you're not alone—hard times come to everyone.

Concern can etch lines into your features and disturb your sleep. Worry balks at the idea of adventure. But if you live in the weeds, you'll never have enough bravery to change direction, even when you secretly want to.

God says you don't need to worry about these things.

He's very aware that people have needs (Matthew 6:32), so His command is not just "Quit complaining"—it's a reminder to use your time more productively. When you worry, you stop seeking God and your role in His plan. . .and your adversary loves it.

Your spiritual eyes should be focused on God and the people He loves instead of things like food, drink, and clothing. Each second you spend dwelling on these things only derails your spiritual focus and amplifies your tunnel vision. You are missing out whenever you insist on identifying with small things instead of God's big ideas.

Do small worries ever cause you to miss big opportunities? How might you use your trust in God to have a freer, more fulfilling life?

Be the Man
WITH CORRECTED VISION

I pray that out of his glorious riches he may strengthen you with power through his Spirit in your inner being, so that Christ may dwell in your hearts through faith. And I pray that you, being rooted and established in love, may have power, together with all the Lord's holy people, to grasp how wide and long and high and deep is the love of Christ, and to know this love that surpasses knowledge—that you may be filled to the measure of all the fullness of God.

EPHESIANS 3:16–19 NIV

Glasses aren't just a fashion choice. When correctly used, they improve your vision, bringing clarity to your blurry world. Suddenly, you can better read and understand words, and you no longer mistake one object for another. Better eyesight helps you ignore the unimportant and focus on the valuable.

The Bible is instrumental in improving your spiritual vision. It offers clarity that changes perspective, helping you see what you could only guess at before. And once you see where you're going, you have the confidence to walk with improved purpose. The apostle Paul wrote, "In him and through faith in him we may approach God with freedom and confidence" (Ephesians 3:12 NIV).

Paul, who saw his faith as the means of approaching God, wanted readers to know that God's overflowing, abundant and unmatched riches could give them strength when they felt like the last dry leaves hanging onto a tree in early winter.

If you want better eyesight, you have to believe glasses can help. Similarly, if you want better spiritual vision, you need to believe the Bible can help. Be a man of courage and read the words of God's great book.

Expect to see things like you never have before.

Is improved spiritual vision important to you? Would a correct understanding of what you see help you make better choices?

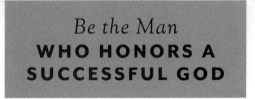

Be the Man
WHO HONORS A
SUCCESSFUL GOD

"Yours, O LORD, is the greatness, the power, the glory, the victory, and the majesty. Everything in the heavens and on earth is yours, O LORD, and this is your kingdom. We adore you as the one who is over all things. Wealth and honor come from you alone, for you rule over everything. Power and might are in your hand, and at your discretion people are made great and given strength."

1 CHRONICLES 29:11-12 NLT

Terrance was exceptional at making waffles—each personally developed mix of batter, Vermont maple syrup, and perfect dairy butter from the Swiss Alps produced just the right texture and taste. One day, as Terrance basked in the taste of his waffles with a friend, John exclaimed, "Fine work, Terrance! It's almost as good as Waffle Hut." Terrance's pride balloon was quietly deflated.

Anyone who has ever gained a positive reputation for something eventually learns the same sobering truth that Terrance learned: you can't please everyone.

You will never be wealthier than God. There is no honor greater than the one He deserves. If greatness comes to Terrance because of his perfectly crisp, home-crafted waffles, it will only be because he used ingredients God made first.

Don't forget God when people applaud you. He gave you each of your successes, whether they're big or small. Any victory He gives is meant to propel you forward in your path toward Him.

It's not hard to see your skills as the reason for your success. But while hard work is important, it's always been God who gave you the resources. From the cells that form your body to the mind you use to think, everything belongs to Him.

How are you using His gifts?

Have you ever tried to impress others? Do you often find yourself thoroughly impressed by God?

Be the Man
WHO UNDERSTANDS
SUFFICIENT

Do we begin again to commend ourselves? or need we, as some others, epistles of commendation to you, or letters of commendation from you? Ye are our epistle written in our hearts, known and read of all men: Forasmuch as ye are manifestly declared to be the epistle of Christ ministered by us, written not with ink, but with the Spirit of the living God; not in tables of stone, but in fleshy tables of the heart. And such trust have we through Christ to God-ward: Not that we are sufficient of ourselves to think any thing as of ourselves; but our sufficiency is of God.

2 CORINTHIANS 3:1–5 KJV

Can you will a heart to beat? Can you force a blind eye to see? Can you create something from absolutely nothing? God did. . .and He still does!

You've probably heard the word *insufficient* more often than *sufficient*. If you have insufficient funds in the bank, you don't have enough money to cover your purchase. If you try to land a job with insufficient skills, you won't know how to do required tasks. If you ask a computer to solve a problem for you, it might respond, "Insufficient data." Each of these examples involves a lack of something you need to achieve your goal.

On your own, you don't have enough to meet your every need. Some things are simply outside your wheelhouse of expertise. This is where God shows up and bridges the gap between your abilities and His. When you invite God into your every effort, He'll respond by offering the help you want and the companionship you need.

Only God can be your absolute sufficiency. Nothing else will do.

Does the fact that God is sufficient for you change your attitude toward new opportunities? How might it enhance your courage?

Be the Man
WHO MAKES CONTINGENCY PLANS

Now listen, you who say, "Today or tomorrow we will go to this or that city, spend a year there, carry on business and make money." Why, you do not even know what will happen tomorrow. What is your life? You are a mist that appears for a little while and then vanishes. Instead, you ought to say, "If it is the Lord's will, we will live and do this or that." As it is, you boast in your arrogant schemes. All such boasting is evil.

JAMES 4:13–16 NIV

Walter had big dreams, and he wanted his family and friends to know about them. This man was going to make his mark in the world of newspapers. However, despite Walter's ambitions and skill, his boss turned him away from this path, believing that Walter's interest in creativity was misplaced.

Like the people mentioned in James 4, Walter's vision for his future was based on personal ambition. But when his self-confidence was shattered, he was humble enough to redirect his ambition elsewhere.

Today, you probably know this man as Walt. . .Disney. Could you imagine what the world would be like if this young man had channeled his creativity into writing bylines in a newspaper?

God wants to be your life consultant. He hates to see you waste your time. He knows you, and He knows what you should do.

When you insist on bypassing God's plan in favor of yours, the tension between the two will never leave. A man of courage doesn't hesitate to admit that all his plans are contingent on God's input and redirection.

How can self-confidence lead to pride?
What can you do to ensure that you never
forsake God's plan and pursue your own?

Be the Man
WHO DOES NOTHING AGAINST THE WILL OF GOD

Balak tried again. This time he sent a larger number of even more distinguished officials than those he had sent the first time. They went to Balaam and delivered this message to him: "This is what Balak son of Zippor says: Please don't let anything stop you from coming to help me. I will pay you very well and do whatever you tell me. Just come and curse these people for me!" But Balaam responded to Balak's messengers, "Even if Balak were to give me his palace filled with silver and gold, I would be powerless to do anything against the will of the Lord my God."

NUMBERS 22:15–18 NLT

Today's scripture passage shares a unique story of courage and boldness. When Balak confidently asked Balaam to curse the people of Israel, Balaam boldly agreed, even though he knew it was a bad idea. In the end, a donkey was the only one courageous enough to oppose the idea. The donkey stopped moving and refused to let Balaam complete his foolish errand.

Perhaps the most surprising thing about this story is that Balaam didn't hesitate or act shocked when the donkey spoke. Instead, he became angry at the creature!

Of the three characters, the donkey demonstrated *real* courage by standing for God's plan and direction. The courage of Balak and Balaam, who were attempting to do something that God would not allow, was just foolishness in disguise.

Sometimes, courage comes from unexpected places and arrives in answers that have been hiding in plain sight. So how can you tell it apart from its counterfeits? *Real* courage reminds you that that God is always worth following.

Have you known people who think they're courageous for opposing God's plans? Why is that kind of courage actually foolish?

Be the Man
WHO KNOWS YOUR OPPOSITION ISN'T GOD

If the LORD delight in us, then he will bring us into this land, and give it us; a land which floweth with milk and honey. Only rebel not ye against the LORD, neither fear ye the people of the land; for they are bread for us: their defence is departed from them, and the LORD is with us: fear them not.

NUMBERS 14:8–9 KJV

Imagine this scene: People are criticizing your personality, clothes, or skin color. They don't like your name, workplace, or opinions. And because they just don't like you much, they make life hard for you.

Those kinds of people have always been a part of life. Your parents, grandparents, and all of your ancestors knew them long before you did.

The Bible is full of stories about opposition. David would one day be king, but before that happened, King Saul tried his best to kill him (1 Samuel 19). Nehemiah rebuilt the walls of Jerusalem, but his enemies showed up in force and tried to stop him (Nehemiah 4). John the

Baptist was opposed by King Herod (Mark 6:14–29), and Stephen was opposed by the local religious elite of his day (Acts 7:54–60). In each case, the opposition sought the demise of good people.

God, however, told these men, "I am with you. Don't fear the opposition." Because no one had been able to oppose God and win, courage made more sense than fear. This message for the people of Israel is for you too. You don't need to fear anything that God is not afraid of.

Men of courage leave fear behind.

What are you afraid of? How can you use the courage that God provides to conquer this fear?

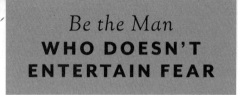

Be the Man
WHO DOESN'T
ENTERTAIN FEAR

"Don't be afraid, for I am with you. Don't be discouraged, for I am your God. I will strengthen you and help you. I will hold you up with my victorious right hand. See, all your angry enemies lie there, confused and humiliated. Anyone who opposes you will die and come to nothing. You will look in vain for those who tried to conquer you. Those who attack you will come to nothing. For I hold you by your right hand—I, the LORD your God. And I say to you, 'Don't be afraid. I am here to help you.'"

ISAIAH 41:10–13 NLT

Every father remembers a time when nightmares chased the sleep from his child. . .who in turn chased the sleep from Dad. The father undoubtedly lifted his kid into bed or walked her back to her room with a firm, gentle reassurance. *Maybe the rest of the night will be different*, Dad hoped. *Maybe sleep will return.*

It's important to remember that fear is a universal emotion—for small children but also for grown men.

Dark nights and bad dreams can inspire it, but your imagination is the worst offender. Fear, however, is not entertained by courage—it's intimidated by it.

Fear is always trying to chase courage from the room. It shows up shouting and thumping its chest, but courage says, "I don't think so!" Suddenly, fear's punch seems like little more than the futile bragging of a bully.

Don't leave home without courage—it's your "fear shield." Don't back up when the only way out is straight ahead. You have a God who renders fear toothless.

Fear is the tail; courage is the head. Which one will you choose?

How can entertaining fear hurt your progress as a Christian? How can courage be the antidote to the fear you encounter today?

Be the Man
WHO WALKS IN ASSURANCE

Moses summoned Joshua and said to him in the presence of all Israel, "Be strong and courageous, for you must go with this people into the land that the LORD swore to their ancestors to give them, and you must divide it among them as their inheritance. The LORD himself goes before you and will be with you; he will never leave you nor forsake you. Do not be afraid; do not be discouraged."

DEUTERONOMY 31:7-8 NIV

The crowd eagerly awaits the entrance of a high official. But before this person arrives, men in black jackets and sunglasses walk in and "sweep the room," looking for anyone who might have a weapon. Once they leave, the VIP can enter the room without fear.

Wouldn't it be nice to have that level of protection? Well, you do! Because God protects His children, you can be a man of courage, knowing with absolute certainty that God has swept the room and taken care of any threats. You'll still encounter difficulty, but this protector walks with you inside the trouble zone. He "works for the good of those who love him, who have been called according to his purpose" (Romans 8:28 NIV).

You'll never have abandonment issues with God. He lives where you live, walks where you walk, and knows what you know. This knowledge should leave you with nothing to frighten or discourage you.

Today, walk forward with the confidence that God's plans will move you beyond any trouble you see. . .or simply imagine.

Do you ever worry that God somehow doesn't know about your troubles? How can you dispel this irrational fear and remember that God has already swept the room?

Be the Man
WHO LEAVES HATE BEHIND

"I tell you the truth, I am the gate for the sheep. All who came before me were thieves and robbers. But the true sheep did not listen to them. Yes, I am the gate. Those who come in through me will be saved. They will come and go freely and will find good pastures. The thief's purpose is to steal and kill and destroy. My purpose is to give them a rich and satisfying life."

JOHN 10:6-10 NLT

People captured during wartime often have harrowing stories to tell. During World War II, people like Louis Zamperini, Olympic runner turned American bomber crew member, and Corrie ten Boom, a Dutch watchmaker who hid Jews in her home, experienced the horrors of Japanese and German prison camps, respectively.

When they were finally released, they had a choice to make: they could spend the rest of their lives hating their captors, or they could forgive and walk into a rich and satisfying life with God.

Satan wants to hold you captive in his own prison of anger and revenge while he destroys everything you love.

He hopes you'll be so filled with anger and revenge that these emotions destroy your life.

God, however, chooses to redeem, repair, and restore. When Jesus died on a cross to rescue you, His final words were "Father, forgive them, for they don't know what they are doing" (Luke 23:34 NLT).

God wants an abundant life for you that rejects anger, retaliation, and anything else that's not conducive to new life. A man of courage will pass his worthless mass of hurt, anger, frustration, and pain to the God who knows what to do with it. And then you'll leave it in God's very capable hands.

Why do people tend to crave revenge as a form of fairness? What would your life be like if God gave you what you deserved?

Be the Man
WHO IS CONTENT TO WAIT

You, therefore, have no excuse, you who pass judgment on someone else, for at whatever point you judge another, you are condemning yourself, because you who pass judgment do the same things. Now we know that God's judgment against those who do such things is based on truth. So when you, a mere human being, pass judgment on them and yet do the same things, do you think you will escape God's judgment? Or do you show contempt for the riches of his kindness, forbearance and patience, not realizing that God's kindness is intended to lead you to repentance?

ROMANS 2:1–4 NIV

Don't you wish that the violent and greedy were banished from modern society? *Why*, you might wonder, *doesn't God do something about it?* There is, after all, a standard of right and wrong—and so many people are clearly in the wrong. Yet the Bible states plainly that everyone (including you) will sin. Evil men as well as good men break His laws.

So when God shows mercy, you should rejoice! Don't get mad at God for showing other sinners the same kindness He's shown you.

Men of courage view God's kindness as a great equalizer. Some people are stubborn, and it's God's kindness (not vengeance) that softens the hardest heart. Ezekiel 36:26 (NIV) explains this process: "I will give you a new heart and put a new spirit in you; I will remove from you your heart of stone and give you a heart of flesh."

Embrace the courage to love imperfect people. Don't follow their example, but follow God's example by believing that anyone can be redeemed. God is still at work among hard men, and the outcome can't be rushed. You can rest assured that your patience will pay off and many men will come to Him.

That's today's good news.

How can you be patient and compassionate
to "lost causes"? What change has
God's kindness made in you?

Be the Man
WHO SEES STRUGGLE AS VALUABLE

The LORD is my light and my salvation; whom shall I fear? the LORD is the strength of my life; of whom shall I be afraid? When the wicked, even mine enemies and my foes, came upon me to eat up my flesh, they stumbled and fell. Though an host should encamp against me, my heart shall not fear: though war should rise against me, in this will I be confident.

PSALM 27:1–3 KJV

Reading Psalm 27, with its numerous examples of God's goodness, not only inspires courage but invites praise.

Here is a quick summary: There's no enemy that needs to be feared (verse 1). Communication with God is important (verse 4). You are protected by God (verse 5), so He's worthy of your praise (verse 6). When you need help, God hears and answers (verse 7). He can teach you how to withstand the enemy (verse 11). Courage comes when you believe in God's goodness (verse 13) and patiently wait on Him (verse 14).

God knows that blocking your struggles won't produce

courage, but He does stand with you as they arrive. If we had nothing to overcome, no enemy to encounter, and no fear to eliminate, why would we ever need courage or the armor of God (see Ephesians 6:10–18)? Patience isn't necessary when everyone agrees with you, and there's no need for an endurance test when everything is perfect.

You should never place your courage in anything other than God—He is good, patient, and wise. You can rest assured that He's orchestrating good outcomes in each bad situation.

Why do you think God allows difficult circumstances to occur? How can you incorporate Psalm 27 into a courageous life?

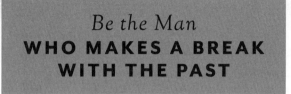

Be the Man
WHO MAKES A BREAK WITH THE PAST

Moses told the people, "Don't be afraid. Just stand still and watch the LORD rescue you today. The Egyptians you see today will never be seen again."

EXODUS 14:13 NLT

The people of Israel had come to Egypt as guests when a famine struck their land. Over time, however, subsequent Pharaohs began treating the Hebrews as slaves and forbidding them to leave. So when God sent Moses to lead the people out, Pharaoh had no intention of complying.

Ten plagues changed his mind. The Israelites were happy to leave, and the Egyptians were happy to see them go. But suddenly, once it occurred to Pharaoh that his country no longer had the support of the Israelites' forced labor, he sent troops to bring the slaves back.

The slaves needed courage. An uncrossable sea stretched in front of them, and an army of horses and chariots thundered behind. Moses consulted God, who then split the sea down the middle, leaving a dry path for hundreds of thousands of people to take.

Even after witnessing this miracle, however, the Hebrews would take a while to abandon their slave mentality.

You might feel this way sometimes. As you walk in the new life God gave you, your old life keeps calling you back. Sometimes, you might even start viewing your sinful past through the deceptive lens of nostalgia.

That's when you must stand still and pay attention. God has rescued you from slavery—why on earth would you return?

How often do you think about returning to your old lifestyle? Why does it take courage to wait on God to remove obstacles that seem too big?

Be the Man
WHO KNOWS THE VALUE
OF A KIND WORD

Anxiety weighs down the heart, but a kind word cheers it up. The righteous choose their friends carefully, but the way of the wicked leads them astray.

PROVERBS 12:25–26 NIV

Dale—an elderly, retired man—had a mission in life: helping children learn to swim. Every afternoon, he stood in the waist-deep section of the local pool as children swarmed to visit him. He always brought a waterproof bag filled with coins that he would scatter across the pool's floor, encouraging the children to practice swimming underwater to retrieve them. Along the way, he offered plenty of guidance and praise.

His dedication did not go unnoticed: eventually, this municipal pool was renamed for Dale.

Would parents have felt as kindly about Dale if he had asked their children to swim with weights around their ankles? That would have restricted their freedom of movement, making it hard to stay afloat and leaving them at an obvious disadvantage.

For grown-up guys, "swimming" in a sea of jobs, relationships, and societal craziness, anxiety can attach weights to your ankles. . .and toss you into the deep end of the pool. Stress and fear can leave you gasping for air, your lungs on fire. God, however, uses Dale's strategy: He offers encouraging words that inspire you to step out in faith, swimming beyond your comfort zone in search for His blessings.

What kind of encouraging words? How about, "God demonstrates his own love for us in this: While we were still sinners, Christ died for us" (Romans 5:8 NIV). Or Jesus' promise in John 16:33 (NIV): "I have told you these things, so that in me you may have peace. In this world you will have trouble. But take heart! I have overcome the world"

Is there anything that routinely weighs you down? How has recognizing and accepting God's kindness brought freedom to your spirit?

Be the Man
WHO KNOWS GOD COUNTS HAIRS

Are not two sparrows sold for a farthing? and one of them shall not fall on the ground without your Father. But the very hairs of your head are all numbered. Fear ye not therefore, ye are of more value than many sparrows. Whosoever therefore shall confess me before men, him will I confess also before my Father which is in heaven.

MATTHEW 10:29-32 KJV

A quick search on your computer, phone, or tablet will reveal that the average number of hairs on a human head is one hundred thousand. However, only God knows the exact amount—nobody else has the time to count.

Similarly, if you look online for the price of birds, you might be surprised to find some figures meandering into the thousands. But those are for the colorful and exotic species from around the world. There's one bird that these websites likely won't mention: sparrows. They are so common that they're easy to overlook.

God, however, made the whole world the sparrows'

cage—and He provides an abundance of food for them in the grass, the dirt, and the cracks in the sidewalks. And if God's care extends to both hair counts and the sparrows you see everywhere, how much more extensive must be His care for His human family members?

Today, be the man of courage who's convinced that God loves His own children most.

Have you ever considered that God cares for even the smallest things? How can this information bolster your courage?

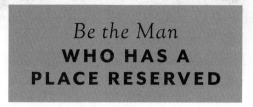

Be the Man
WHO HAS A
PLACE RESERVED

[Jesus said,] "Don't let your hearts be troubled. Trust in God, and trust also in me. There is more than enough room in my Father's home. If this were not so, would I have told you that I am going to prepare a place for you?"

JOHN 14:1-2 NLT

The story of Christmas is probably familiar to you. Jesus wasn't born in the local palace or in the presence of kings. No, He was born in a Bethlehem stable because there was "no lodging available" (Luke 2:7 NLT). While every child is a miracle, Jesus was, to most, just one more in a sea of babies.

Jesus, however, knew things would be this way. His plan was bigger than the notions of the spiritual elite. Because His plan didn't conform to their best guess, Jesus became an outcast to the very men who'd been looking for His arrival their entire lives. He was not welcome here, but His lack of acceptance did not derail His mission or stop Him from welcoming sinners.

He spoke honestly, loved completely, and forgave those who took His life. Long before our planet was created, God began preparing a place for His family. There's more than enough room, and men of courage long to be there.

Refuse to let doubt turn into disbelief. Ask God questions, not as a skeptic but as an eager student who's willing to learn.

God won't hang out a No Vacancy sign—His Son has left a light on just for you. He wants you to find Him.

How can you convert any doubts you entertain into trust? Why did Jesus make room for you even before you became part of His family?

Be the Man
WHO'S WILLING TO
REORGANIZE PRIORITIES

The LORD is my shepherd; I shall not want. He maketh me to lie down in green pastures: he leadeth me beside the still waters. He restoreth my soul: he leadeth me in the paths of righteousness for his name's sake. Yea, though I walk through the valley of the shadow of death, I will fear no evil: for thou art with me; thy rod and thy staff they comfort me. Thou preparest a table before me in the presence of mine enemies: thou anointest my head with oil; my cup runneth over. Surely goodness and mercy shall follow me all the days of my life: and I will dwell in the house of the LORD for ever.

PSALM 23:1-6 KJV

Young people focus on everything they want to accomplish in a career. They have dreams, aspirations, and ideas they want to explore. During this invigorating time in life, it's hard to accept that anything is impossible. By middle age, however, doubts start creeping in about the importance of everything you sought to achieve. As you continue to mature, your priorities begin to shift. You started bold, but your boldness is gradually turning to *courage*. Eventually, your long-term goals lead to a different place entirely.

If you've been paying attention, then you've seen the fingerprints of God's mercy scattered throughout your life. He's been there in job loss, health crises, and the death of a loved one. When trouble comes, things you thought were important take a back seat, and the truly vital things become job one. Your new, eternal life with God overshadows any of your past achievements.

Today, what will you pay attention to—temporal possessions or God's infinitely better promises?

Have your priorities changed with the passing of time? If so, how have these changes impacted your willingness to follow God?

Be the Man
WHO PRAYS FOR COURAGE. . .
FOR HIMSELF AND
FOR OTHERS

And pray in the Spirit on all occasions with all kinds of prayers and requests. With this in mind, be alert and always keep on praying for all the Lord's people. Pray also for me, that whenever I speak, words may be given me so that I will fearlessly make known the mystery of the gospel, for which I am an ambassador in chains. Pray that I may declare it fearlessly, as I should.

EPHESIANS 6:18-20 NIV

When you ask people to pray for you, do you ask them to pray that God takes your trouble away or that He enables you to endure it?

Both of these are good prayer policies. The apostle Paul struggled tremendously as he followed Jesus. He even asked God three times to remove "a thorn in the flesh" (see 2 Corinthians 12:7 KJV; nobody knows exactly what the "thorn" was). However, in Ephesians 6, Paul also asked people to pray for him so that he could courageously say,

"There's no price I'm unwilling to pay to keep sharing the truth."

Paul called himself an ambassador because he represented Christ to the world. Sometimes, his audience responded with skepticism, hostility, and even violence. Not everyone who heard good news accepted it as such.

You can (and should) pray for God's comfort and relief from the things that are too difficult for you, but don't forget also to pray for the ability to withstand them. Sometimes, God will answer the second prayer before He answers the first.

If you could choose between asking for relief or asking for endurance, which option would you take? Why?

Be the Man
WHO ACCEPTS A COMMISSION

Jesus came and told his disciples, "I have been given all authority in heaven and on earth. Therefore, go and make disciples of all the nations, baptizing them in the name of the Father and the Son and the Holy Spirit. Teach these new disciples to obey all the commands I have given you. And be sure of this: I am with you always, even to the end of the age."

MATTHEW 28:18-20 NLT

You need direction—everyone does. You need an assignment—God gives them to His followers. You may not recognize your mission at first due to its seeming simplicity. It could be holding the door open for someone or politely waving at a grumpy neighbor. These random acts of kindness often make the most impact and can affect a person's life much longer than you might think.

God commissions ambassadors like you to be men of courage who recruit by sharing the truth about the Christian life. You will do everyone a disservice if you declare that Christians never struggle or make mistakes. If you're honest, you easily admit that you have struggles. . .but also that you don't face them alone.

Courage is vital to your commission. You'll go places you wouldn't normally go and talk to people you've never noticed before. God wants to make it clear that He is with you today, tomorrow, and the rest of your existence.

When your struggles come, they will also go. When trouble finds you, God will eventually show it the door. When pain appears, your promised future will one day banish it forever.

Courageous men share this wonderful news to everyone who needs to know.

How can the idea that God has commissioned you motivate you to share your faith? How can you use your struggles to connect with others when talking about God?

MORE DEVOTIONS FOR MEN

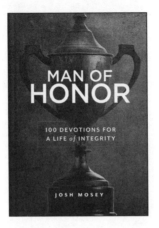

Men, set a powerful example for the world. Be the person God wants you to be with *Man of Honor: 100 Devotions for a Life of Integrity*. Each entry encourages readers to "be the man"—the man who stands for right, values loyalty, defers to God's will, avoids pretense, and serves sacrificially.

Hardcover / 978-1-63609-375-8